MW01199785

A Magnificent
OBSESSION

Danielle Green's book will be a valuable companion to those who have been smitten with a mystical call or a powerful spiritual experience....[S]he makes useful distinctions between religious experience and spiritual, transpersonal experience; and between mystical experience and mystical call....Green interweaves a remarkable (and well-written) personal narrative with solid scholarship that positions her topic historically and interculturally.

Kendra Smith, PhD. Psychologist

In Dr. Green's eloquently written book she manages to capture and share powerful glimpses of the eternal that are rarely seen and often fleetingly experienced. By sharing the stories of everyday people who have been blessed by a mystical realization of their life's purpose, Green opens the heavenly veil for us and invites us into a deeper exploration of who we truly are, why we are here, and what is our ordained purpose.

She asks us to consider, "A non-visible realm lives and breathes in us, through us and around us. Or, perhaps it is we who live and breathe through it?"

And so, Danielle gentle challenges us, coaxes us, points out the sign posts and ultimately guides us through the deeper waters that can lead to our spiritual realization and actualization. In coming to an understanding of her "magnificent obsession" she invites us, the readers, to also accept and identify with the purpose of our soul's journey.

Joan Lowery, M.Ed. Communications Specialist, Writer and Seeker

A Magnificent OBSESSION

MY LIFELONG SEARCH FOR THE MEANING OF A MYSTICAL CALL

Danielle Green, PhD

ARCHWAY
PUBLISHING

Copyright © 2019 Danielle Green, PhD.

All rights reserved. No part of this book may be used or reproduced by any means, graphic, electronic, or mechanical, including photocopying, recording, taping or by any information storage retrieval system without the written permission of the author except in the case of brief quotations embodied in critical articles and reviews.

This book is a work of non-fiction. Unless otherwise noted, the author and the publisher make no explicit guarantees as to the accuracy of the information contained in this book and in some cases, names of people and places have been altered to protect their privacy.

Archway Publishing books may be ordered through booksellers or by contacting:

Archway Publishing
1663 Liberty Drive
Bloomington, IN 47403
www.archwaypublishing.com
1 (888) 242-5904

Because of the dynamic nature of the Internet, any web addresses or links contained in this book may have changed since publication and may no longer be valid. The views expressed in this work are solely those of the author and do not necessarily reflect the views of the publisher, and the publisher hereby disclaims any responsibility for them.

Any people depicted in stock imagery provided by Getty Images are models, and such images are being used for illustrative purposes only. Certain stock imagery © Getty Images.

Cover Image: "The Calling" © Alan S. Maltz/ALANMALTZ.COM

Scripture taken from the King James Version of the Bible.

ISBN: 978-1-4808-7010-9 (sc)
ISBN: 978-1-4808-7009-3 (hc)
ISBN: 978-1-4808-7011-6 (e)

Library of Congress Control Number: 2018965997

Print information available on the last page.

Archway Publishing rev. date: 1/3/2019

Contents

You must say yes or no to the light that you have seen. There are a thousand ways to say no; one way to say yes and no way of saying anything else. It is a tremendous decision.

—Gregory Vlastos, Professor of Philosophy, Emeritus; Princeton University and University of California at Berkeley

Dedication

This manuscript is dedicated to my parents, Daniel and Loretta Louise Green, whose steadfast love and practical support made it possible for me to fulfill my own call to conduct this final study.

I am, and will always be, grateful for my patient and beautiful daughters, Hadley and Annaporva, who have inspired and blessed me in unspeakable ways; and with whom I share my love affair with the Divine. Your childhoods have been shaped by my determination to understand mystical calls and the practical family sacrifices made to write this book. I accepted Maya Angelou's warning that no agony is greater than that of the untold story living inside. May this work serve as a reminder to honor your unique calls, voice them freely, and live them with courage as we travel this wild and gentle planet.

Preface

Perhaps every soul enters the world knowing that it is unalterably corded to an invisible world, but in adapting to physical form, forgets. And perhaps the entire life span is a process of remembering and forgetting until one is seized by an experience in which the veil is momentarily lifted—and that which was once easily forgotten is sufficiently vivid and is locked into memory.

The book that you have in your hands speaks to such an event, a moment in time in which the great, ever-present Mystery shows itself in the form of a *mystical call*. The mystical call beckons us to awaken to the real story of existence: our invisible bond to this larger reality and our personal destiny, which is imprinted on the soul.

When such an event occurs, even if only fleetingly, our longing is satisfied and we step into a place and know home. Here, the veil of quotidian reality is temporarily lifted and we encounter the infinite, even as we cannot sustain this level of consciousness at this point in the evolution of our species. The cosmos is too vast, our nervous systems are too undeveloped, and our cognition too unformed to have more than a glimpse of such expansive reality.

This is the light that is seen—and once seen, changes everything. While the nature of mysticism is essentially immeasurable and inexpressible in everyday language, it is hoped that the following pages will provide a deeper understanding of a particular type of mystical experience, that which is marked by a spiritual encounter, resulting in a specific life assignment.

From an early age in my life, this subject has been a magnificent obsession. What is a mystical call? What does it mean to be called? How does one recognize if it happens? What similarities are shared among those called around the globe and through time? What are various individuals called to do—and why?

These driving questions have absorbed me since childhood. They propelled me through my studies in seminary, my clinical practice as a psychotherapist and psychoanalyst, and finally, in the finished work of a dissertation. The backbone of *Magnificent Obsession* is that dissertation, written nearly two decades ago in a significantly different chapter of my life. Nevertheless, the essence of its subject remains a central theme and driving passion and consequently, has propelled me to review, update, and edit the material for the lay reader. This is research that in its purest form began in childhood and was completed well into adulthood.

My pilgrimage has carried me across continents and through many cultures and religious traditions in my search for others who have been driven by the mystical call. Typically, those of us who have experienced such a call have recognized each other, making it possible to support each other and share in the mystery wrapped in each call. In full voice and in hushed tones, shared in joy as well as fear, brave peoples' stories have made it possible to inch closer to an answer.

The following life stories include narratives from individuals ranging in age from three to ninety-three years old and represent many world traditions and spiritual orientations, including Roman Catholic, Protestant, Jew, Muslim, Buddhist, and Hindu; "spiritual, but not religious"; no religion or spiritual orientation or affiliation; agnostic; and atheist. The subjects hail from the United States, United Kingdom, South Africa, Asia, and Australia.

Individuals have been given pseudonyms; some of their most notable personal characteristics have been disguised and identifying details scrambled. Some stories stand alone, while others house a composite of several narratives in an effort to mask identities yet capture the essence of the shared experience. Except for statements marked by quotations, the stories are paraphrased for brevity as well as emphasis.

This inquiry was not merely an intellectual pursuit, but a desperate attempt to understand my own interactions. I could not "not" complete this assignment. This work is an act of self-preservation, an effort to solve the riddle of my own mystical excursions. It has fed my need to find kinship with those who know this constant coaxing from the invisible world and help those who are struggling to listen, stop, and heed the call.

Essentially, my own call would not be complete if I didn't write this book. There are several exemplary bodies of work in different disciplines on the phenomena of the call, but no collection in written literature to date combines contemporary stories of the *mystical call*, researches their rich historical lineage, identifies shared characteristics, examines its impact and after-effects, identifies the call's assignments, and unpacks a psychological interpretation of the experience. To that end, I have written what I need to read.

Maybe you picked up this book to probe the nature of your own mystical experiences or to understand a particular experience that occurred recently, or long ago. Or are you trying to make sense of an assignment that you accepted or denied, and wonder what the unlived call may have shown you in your life? It takes courage to face the unknown spiritual domain. The journey into consciousness is rarely a smooth passage. It requires a willingness to surrender to a larger mystery - an everyday act of faith in a fear-driven world.

As the following stories speak, it becomes apparent that humans are wrestling with the angels of destiny, summoning us to a larger vision that has marked human history and contributes to the evolution of consciousness. Spirituality is as ancient as human history itself, and although this vast knowing can be easily lost in a culture shaped by industrial greed, rampant superficialities, and ego-driven desires, the mystical call reminds us that the sacred world is eternal, always extending an outstretched hand.

PART I

Dual Citizenship

CHAPTER 1

Human beings do not stand in one world only but between two worlds and must distinguish themselves from their functions in both worlds. You have to stand between the gods and men. —Carl Jung

My earliest memory, less than age four, is of a distinctly mystical experience. Looking back on it today, I seemed to have an acute awareness of the invisible world. Was it merely a child's imagination? Or did it reflect life in seemingly dual, coexisting realms, even if such duality is an illusion?

My father, aged twenty-four, drove a Sunbeam truck. He delivered bread through the small towns of rural southern Ohio. This day, he was going to let us ride along, even though it meant waking long before dawn, four-thirty they'd said. I was eager for this time with Dad, and at bedtime the night before, my sister and I talked about playing among the large metal racks of trays, basking in the rich scent of freshly baked bread, cakes, and pies along the route. As I remained dozing in bed in the still dark morning, I could hear my parents murmuring about the weather as my mother dressed my older sister in winter layers, suitable for riding in the back of the large bread truck.

In my drowsy state, I absorbed the usual morning conversation between my parents, but then it faded as I heard another voice. This voice was a hushed whisper, and I could feel a soft breeze as the instructive words entered my young consciousness, *Do not open your eyes. Keep them closed. It is important that you do not move. Let them think that you are sound asleep. Do not go today. Do not let your family go today. Stay still and wait.*

I stayed very still, my eyes gently closed as my parents tried to rally me, first my mother and then both of them gently rocking me. After several of their futile attempts, I heard my mother lament that I might be too tired from yesterday's activities to rise this early. Repeating my name, she continued to pat me. I turned away from the touch of her warm hand, torn between her intention and the angel's instruction. I waited and listened. My parents stood over me, confused and exasperated as I continued to appear limp with sleep. They turned off the bedroom light and I heard them recede down the hallway to the kitchen. Moments later, the storm door slammed shut and then came the crunching footsteps of my father as he braved another dark, frozen morning. Slowly, I let out a sigh of relief and began to breathe normally. The soft presence lifted and disappeared.

It was only later that I understood the import of the message. On a rural, icy road, my father's vehicle flipped when heading around a sharp curve, landing in a cornfield. My dad held on to the steering wheel for dear life, rolling with the truck. Crawling out through the broken windshield, he escaped with minor cuts and bruises.

This was before the days of seatbelts. My mother in the passenger seat would not have fared as well, nor my sister and me, standing without seats among the tall, oversized racks. The bread trays flew about as the truck spun and rolled across the icy road, before it landed upside down in a pool of glass in the nearby field.

Early memories make a strong impression. As a trained thera-pist, I can think of many things about which I'd say *Gosh, memory is slippery, I don't know*, but this I do. I remember being on the bed. Listening to my parents talk. For some reason, I remembered it very, very clearly, and this overwhelming sense of relief that we didn't go. And a greater sense of relief when I realized all that hap-pened to my dad—he came home pretty beaten up.

This event captures what I call *dual citizenship*: conscious practicalities driving our days one moment; messages from the invisible world reaching out to us in another. We live in these physical bodies that need all this care and attention, yet our reality is vaster than what can be absorbed with the ra-tional mind. A non-visible realm lives and breathes in us, through us, and around us. Or perhaps it is we who live and breathe through it?

This world "more real than real"—a term coined by Jungian analyst Robert A. Johnson—is always revealing itself to the listen-ing heart.

Understanding the Word

What is the meaning of being *called*? How can we comprehend this kind of non-rational experience psychologically? Although the study of mysticism has overlapped with many academic fields—including anthropology, art, mythology, wisdom traditions, philosophy and religious studies—very little in the field of psychology is provided. The notable exceptions are the work of William James and Carl Jung.

People speak of being "called" to, say, become a teacher; or that, after many years, they've finally found their "calling." The field of career counseling borrowed the term *call* from religious studies in the second half of the twentieth century. From there, the notion slipped into contemporary parlance to connote a heightened emotional response or intuitive hunch, as in "I felt it was my *calling* to rescue that puppy"—or even, "the cookie jar just *called* to me."

The classical and historic meaning is found in ancient religious and mystical contexts. In the Old and New Testaments, the term *calling* is referenced in some form over seven hundred times. It is derived from the Hebrew root *gr* and the Greek word *klesis*, meaning "to call, summon." In the Old Testament, callings refer to the direct relationship between God and his people.

When I began this study, there were no existing cross-cultural studies as to the psychology of *mystical calls*, a term I coined to distinguish a mystical experience from a mystical call, the latter of which includes the assignment of a life task. Only two psychological interpretations were applicable: William James' psychology of religious experiences and Carl Jung's study of archetypes and the unconscious, which provides the framework to interpret what actually happens during a mystical event. It is upon their psychological shoulders that I stand.

The Call and the Archetype

Jung's recognition of the mystical grew out of his own passion for self-understanding and a willingness to penetrate, and be penetrated by, the invisible world—pools of swirling energy patterns he recognized as *archetypes*.

Archetypes are defined in Jungian literature as the cumulative wisdom that is transmitted genetically and mediated by our psychological development and nervous systems. When an archetype is activated, it is an influence that is always operating in one's life and must be adequately integrated into the psyche and normal waking consciousness. Archetypes provide a template for living within universal and identifiable motifs and themes: *mother, hero, child, magician* are a few of the more common. While universal in recognition, they are simultaneously unique in each person's experience and interpretation. Hence, an archetype's influence shows differently in each consciousness. While we all recognize the mother archetype, one person may experience the universal mother as compassion and nurture; another may experience her as an intrusive, controlling figure. The former will lead to comfort, vitality and energy; the latter to an unhealthy internalization of the mother as a negative association. This dysfunction results in an inner battle to manage the enormity of the dark mother complex. Understanding one's relationship with prevailing archetypal influences is critical for self-understanding.

Jung believed that the mystical call occurs when an individual is seized by the archetype. A close encounter with an archetype is both physiologically and psychologically powerful. This marks a person in such a life-determining way that a shift in consciousness is generated, serving as an initiation to a larger life. From this point, the individual sets off on the journey towards *individuation*, a concept described as a process of self-actualization, awakening, or becoming conscious. Regardless of the term used, according to Jung, the *call* is an event that pulls one toward destiny, which begins and ends with being present to one's true essential Self and fulfilling a vocational duty. The transformational process has begun.

Ardent Religiosity
and the Mystical Call

CHAPTER 2

*I saw the Lord sitting upon a throne, ... and his train
filled the temple ... I heard the voice of the Lord
saying, "Whom shall we send?" Then I said, "Here
am I, send me."* —Isaiah 6:1–8

As **a child, I was** possessed by a magnificent presence, something I could only call God. This steadfast perception was an abiding source of comfort, joy, and security throughout my early years in Springfield, Ohio. Gripped by this presence, I longed to hear the stories of old, learn scripture, and pray. Enthralled by everything that spoke of a divine source—and terribly bored by perfunctory learning that ignored the invisible world—I wondered how my first-grade teacher could bear teaching such irrelevance, taking all this alphabet stuff so seriously. Wouldn't Mrs. Bobo rather teach the great mysteries of God? Or was it possible that Mrs. Bobo did not know what I knew?

I was eager to go anywhere to learn about God, so attending services several times a week with my actively churchgoing family was right up my alley. The Assembly of God, a Pentecostal congregation, offered a community eager to speak of religious matters, even as the centerpiece was a rigid message of right-or-wrong, sin-or-salvation. Getting saved, staying saved, and dying saved were its cornerstones, and since backsliding was easy and the rapture as predicted in the book of Revelation could occur anytime—whisking the saved off to heaven and leaving everyone else to burn in hell—we all had to stay vigilant to follow biblical teaching (as taught by the Assembly of God Church).

Sunday morning and evening services, along with Wednesday evening prayer meetings, and special services whenever the preacher believed the church was in need of "revival," found me dressed and waiting in the family 1957 two-toned green Buick to head through the winding countryside. Once there, I could ask questions about the Bible, sing hymns, and feel the presence of angels around me.

And then, after years of membership, my parents left the church for reasons I believed had everything to do with my mother's determination to wear red lipstick.

Expanding the Image of God

My earliest memory of witnessing a rebellious act, standing up to authority, and using your body to defy oppressive doctrine occurred in the pew of the Assembly of God.

The women were always making comments about Mother's lipstick, something that was unacceptable in the Pentecostal church. Cozying up against my mother during a Sunday evening altar call, I recall the organist Libby pausing as the congregation droned on, singing *Just As I Am*. Stepping down from the chancel, she made her way to our row and squeezed in, speaking with my mother in hushed tones, asking her to give up "that stuff you wear on your lips and give your life to the Lord." My mother didn't actually walk out, although I imagined it that way. Intuitively, I knew it was *over* and wrote my first poem about it.

To my child's ear, the slamming of the Pentecostal doors, meta-phorical or not, rang loudly, and preceded a long march across town to the Calvary Baptist Church, where the women wore makeup and the youth group was allowed to attend (some) movies and listen to the Beatles on their transistor radios.

Click, Click, Slam

Not even the full-voiced,
hypnotic repetition of the altar calls,
"Just as I am without one plea
but that thy blood was shed
    for me
and that thou bidst me come
    to thee,
I come, I come,"
could drown out the
click, click, slam
of that sharp,
self-determining,
no-turning-back act
of my mother's.

With the last resounding,
near-deafening bang
of those church doors
on my young ears
on that hot, sultry
July Kentucky night,
they came to the altar,
and she went.
Click, Click, Slam.

Overlaying lapping sounds
and images
blurring, flashing,
freezing me in time
as fat, fat rolls of Libby Lucy
    Jane's
old, worn fat unravels itself
from the oversized organ,
dwarfed by teeming mounds
    of flesh.
And Libby Lucy Jane waddles,
rocking, rolling
down the chancel steps
to my mother's till-now timid
    self.
Click, Click, Slam.

I sit next to my mother, glanc-
    ing up
for all but an eternal second,
forever to see Libby Lucy Jane's
    third chin
jitterbugging on her clavicle

as she peers with her
    pseudo-compassionate,
pseudo-sweet,
pseudo-Christian,
singsong voice.
Click, Click, Slam.

Dizzily, I make out Libby Lucy
    Jane's
pale-faced, frozen lips declaring,
"Loretta Louise, why don't you
wipe off that red stuff,
come to the altar,
and turn your life over to the
    Lord?"
Click, Click, Slam,

The heat rose with my mother
on that mid-July night
as the choir crooned on,
"I come, I come."
And my mother went,
Red-lipped and all,
Click, Click, Slam.

Risking my Father God's wrath
and hellfire itself,
those proud red lips went out
into the lightning bug's glow
Of night's freedom.

Mother (or Mommie as I always called her) unknowingly provided a framework for me to envision a bigger spirit than the small God that shapes most conservative traditions. It was my first glimpse of a free God. Although my parents shut the door on that church's narrow sense of morality, I did find my way back to the Pentecostals through the years, and sought out many other churches as well. I attended every summer Bible school I could get to, sneaked into Catholic masses, and read daily scripture. I entered—and won—every Bible contest I could find.

I was riveted by the Old Testament stories and the struggle of the Jewish people. When a friend of mine reported that she knew a Jewish girl, exceedingly rare in Springfield, an electric wave of excitement shot through my young body. I felt an uncanny identification and had an urge to claim, "That's me!" This marked the beginning of my interest in Judaism and, in time, a growing interest in all faiths and traditions. I wanted to be as close to God as possible, and the more lenses through which I could see God, the better.

My father disapproved of my involvement with so many different churches and heatedly wailed, "You're going to grow up confused!" Not only did I not feel confused, I felt more alive—as if a deeper connection to the Source was breathing in and through me. (Neither my father nor I knew this was fertile ground for the makings of a Unitarian Universalist minister.)

My First Mystical Call

At age ten, I attended Camp Chaffee, a summer sleepaway Bible camp affiliated with our new American Baptist church. One night, at vespers, while dancing fireflies lit the muggy July darkness and we campers sat silently by the lakeside, I heard a voice speak out. It was definitively not coming from any of the little girls. In that moment, a shadowy outlined figure came to me. saying the words, "give your life to service... go forth into the world and preach the gospel to every creature."

Initially, I was scared of the vision and the deep voice ringing through the darkness, but I recognized it as the warm presence I called God. A wave of love carried me to a serene place and quieted my fears. Again, I heard the voice call out: "go forth into the world and preach the gospel, the news of love to every creature." My heart leapt in my ten-year-old chest. I was unable to move or speak and, as with the other instruction I had received as a preschooler, I waited. Time stood still, or perhaps it no longer existed. Everything was suspended in space as I listened for further instructions. But nothing came except the sound of shuffling feet, as young campers headed back to their nearby cabins.

It was my first mystical call, by definition a visitation with a message about my life's purpose. This far surpassed all religious experiences that I had known to date, including trembling with joy while speaking in tongues at the Assembly of God church, or waiting in breathless anticipation to witness the miracle at the summer tent revival meetings. There I'd sit preening above the crowd, on my young father's strong shoulders, as Oral Roberts poured oil on those pleading for healing as they swayed, trance-like, before the altar. No, this message was an instruction, and an encounter with a transcendent entity that I had not known before. I felt transported to another place and time.

As I returned to my cabin, my mood morphed to panic. What had just happened? What did this mean? Certainly, it didn't mean that I was called to be a preacher, as girls weren't pastors. Did it mean that I was called to be a missionary? The very thought frightened me. I felt small and powerless in the face of God's instruction. I also felt betrayed. Why would God want me to do something I didn't want to do? Now I would have to choose between living the life of my own making and the will of God. I imagined that I would be called to work in a faraway place like India, which held no interest for me. Curiously, each time I closed my eyes, I saw what I believed were East Indian people standing before me—although to the best of my knowledge, I had never seen an Asian person. My thoughts raced to the Bible stories about those, like Jonah, who were called to serve, but refused to listen. Fearful that I would be like one of those who sought God, but when encountered, was powerless, I climbed into my cabin bunk and hoped that the other girls did not hear me as I cried myself to sleep.

I awoke the following day tired and disoriented, trying to forget the events of the previous night as I went about my morning chores. It was then that Mrs. Carol, a middle-aged pastor's wife in plaid Bermuda shorts approached me. She asked if she could speak with me about her experience at vespers the night before. I was in no mood to talk about vespers and could hardly recall the peace or bath of love that flooded me before and immediately following the voice. All I could think about was that I was headed for a jungle in India.

But never one to disobey adults, I followed Mrs. Carol to the cabin while the other campers went to their assigned activities. In the quiet of the cabin, usually bustling with twelve chatty girls, Mrs. Carol began to tell me that God had spoken to her during prayer at vespers the previous evening. He had told her that I was called to be of service to him. She said that God had instructed her to speak with me so that I would understand the call and surrender to his guidance. Mrs. Carol was startled by this message and afraid of upsetting me, but she knew she had to follow God's instruction, reminding me, "God works in mysterious ways." Sitting by my side on the lumpy bunk bed, she carefully placed her arm around my shoulder and assured me that God would never lead us astray. Her deep-set brown eyes rested on mine as she reassured me that if I surrendered to God's call everything would work out better than anything I could imagine.

Through tearful fits and starts, I told her how I knew God had called me and I wanted to do what was right but I wasn't sure I wanted to be a missionary and journey to a country by myself. On Mrs. Carol's comforting shoulder, my fears were allayed as she prayed and rocked me, encouraging me to say yes to God and trust that in due time, I would understand this call, the nature of what I was meant to do, and receive all the help I needed to fulfill it.

As days turned into months, I surrendered to the fact that I would be a missionary because I did not know any other way to interpret "his service." I read missionary stories, contacted a missionary group through my church to enlist a daughter of one of the missionaries to become my pen pal, designed and facilitated a monthly "Missionary Sunday" church program to learn about missionaries, and led church services at local nursing homes. I can only imagine the nursing staff's surprise when a billed "midweek special service" was a skinny ten-year-old one-person band. I read scripture, preached, played the piano and sang as the frail, largely wheelchair-bound group nodded off to my carefully prepared service.

In time, I grew to accept that this was to be my life's work. I was never the same. I no longer dreamed of the life I once envisioned: a husband, children, teaching elementary school in southern Ohio and having my own Sunday school class. Now, I saw myself in India, working with the poor, teaching children and married to a minister, if married at all. This one childhood experience, in all its innocence, has largely shaped my life, even as the interpretation of what it meant evolved through the years. Here, in these early experiences, my destiny was calling.

Do You Hear
What I Hear?

CHAPTER 3

When Laurens van der Post one night in the Kalahari
Desert told the Bushmen he couldn't hear the stars
singing, they didn't believe him. They looked at him,
half-smiling. They examined his face to see whether
he was joking or deceiving them. Then two of those
small men who plant nothing, who have almost
nothing to hunt, who live on almost nothing, and
with no one but themselves, led him away from the
crackling thorn-scrub fire and stood with him under
the night sky and listened. Do you not hear them
now? And van der Post listened, not wanting to dis-
believe, but had to say No. They walked him slowly
like a sick man to the small dim circle of firelight
and told that they were sorry ...
    —*David Wagoner*, The Silence of the Stars

The tragic inattention paid to the cosmos by modern men
and women is captured in the story of British philosopher
Laurens van der Post, when he laments his inability to hear the stars
singing and blames his ancestors for what they have lost—a void
that now becomes his own. In some ways, the sensory experience

of soulful living is reclaimed when one is touched by the mystical. As one's very neurons awake, an ancient yet brand new life map appears. More is possible.

Through the nature of the sensory mystical call, the larger cosmos speaks, and in so doing, a map of one's fundamental orientation to work and destiny shows itself. And for many, as in my own childhood, the constellations sang, and plants and animals spoke. In childhood, I didn't feel the need for a conceptual or intellectual understanding—I just wanted to be a good listener and servant of this grand invisible cosmos.

Leaving the Garden of Eden

Before I knew differently, I presumed everyone received guidance, heard voices, spoke in tongues, and participated in an invisible Mystery. That is, until I was about nine years old and discovered that my classmates didn't. These series of revelations, and one event in particular, changed my notion of myself and who or what I was, or could be. I lost my footing in the safe circle of childhood friends.

I was in the fourth grade when I noticed that other children were not daydreaming about God and how they could serve him. Their diaries were not documenting the daily miracles of grade school. My friends not only didn't speak in tongues during their evening prayers; they were not even praying—except maybe before a test, or when they feared they were in trouble, or when they heard their parents fight. They certainly were not attending prayer meetings and pouring warm oil on the sick and disheartened.

At first, like the Bushmen's response to Laurens van der Post, I was in disbelief that they did not hear God during recess. Were they goofing on me? Or did they want to keep their treasured divine messages a secret from me? Sometime, between the changing leaves and the last bell marking summer break, I realized that my friends did not know what I was talking about and, furthermore, were not particularly interested.

Before that moment of reckoning, however, I was sure that my peers simply did not understand. Perhaps language was at fault: we used different terminology to describe our respective experiences. Maybe they felt another sensation when touching sick animals or friends, unlike the hot tingling that I knew. I imagined that spiritual gifts were manifested differently to each person—and that, in time, I would learn about the unique experiences of my classmates. I recall wondering if the states of ecstasy I knew, accompanied by gibberish-like words when enraptured in prayer at the altar, happened elsewhere to my friends. Did they discover God while working in the barn, gathering vegetables in the garden, playing in the swimming hole?

Poet Mary Oliver has confessed, "I don't know exactly what a prayer is. I do know how to pay attention, how to fall down into the grass, how to kneel down in the grass, how to be idle and blessed, and how to stroll through the fields ..." Surely my friends had their methods of paying attention to the sacred world. In time, I would understand it.

Whatever self-doubt lingered, it was clarified at Susie Miller's tenth birthday party. Wrapped in sleeping bags in her backyard tent, amidst gales and giggles, we confessed to boy-crushes, revealed our favorite band member in The Monkees, and admitted our private horror fantasies about our fourth-grade teacher Mrs. Bull, who rightly lived up to her name.

Susie turned the subject to the popular TV show, *Bewitched*. She said Samantha, the witch played by Elizabeth Montgomery, could make our boy-dreams come true, bring The Monkees to our school, or break Mrs. Bull's long skinny legs, leaving it impossible for her to wear the necessary plaster casts under her tight pencil skirts. With Mrs. Bull restricted to a long homebound period of recuperation, we would be free to roam the halls, chew gum, flirt with boys, and crank up the music in class. As giggles erupted to wild roars, Susie turned her attention to me. She suggested that I could manifest this fantasy, since weird witchy things were always happening around me. Laughter morphed into teasing jabs.

"Think you could wave your wand and replace Mrs. Bull with Mrs. Williams, that kindergarten teacher who brings cookies?" one shouted.

"Do you pretend to be a mortal when we walk in, like Samantha when Darrin comes home from work?" another inquired.

"Did you use magic when you whispered 'Baby Jesus, lost and found, help me while I look around' and then found Polly's necklace in the swimming hole?"

"Will you be flying away on your broomstick tonight when we fall asleep?"

Fortunately for me, the growing riotous giggles of these grade school girls came to an end when Susie's mom popped her head into the tent to quiet us and announce bedtime.

Slumber descended on the circle of tired girls. That is, on everyone but me. I lay awake staring at the constellations through the open flap and wondered how I could face everyone in the morning light—or more importantly, come to terms with my weirdness. There was something about their innocent teasing that left me feeling "outed," completely alone, left musing about uncanny events and otherworldly communications that I was sure peppered my life from some other realm.

I never forgot Susie's party. I'd suspected my naïve talk of God and miracles meant I was different. But in the hilarity of a birthday party, they believed that I was a witch. My friends were not on my wavelength. It was the end of assuming that I fit in. I knew I didn't.

As I pondered with the limited insight of a ten-year-old, I decided that if I was different, it was a *bad* difference, no doubt confirmed by my older sister's taunting. I wondered if Barbie simply voiced what other kids felt when, as a popular girl, she would bounce past my bedroom door hissing, "How's Little Miss Christian Goody-goody? Are you going to be Perfect today? Read your Bible yet this morning?"

Is this how all the kids saw me, and if they didn't, would they, if they only knew? Somehow, the religious world of my early childhood got entangled with spells and magic and gave me a stamp of "weird," a label that had to be reworked into adulthood.

As my awareness grew, so did my loneliness. I began to spend more time by myself, waiting for the neighbor's horse to approach the nearby fence for treats, or study the cows meandering in the distance, or amble through a small abandoned cemetery. It inspired me to create my own graveyard. Soon, I buried every dead bird, rabbit, squirrel, frog, mouse, kitten, snake, and spider found in the nearby woods or along the country road. Each life received a noteworthy funeral service, attended by the family dogs and cats, while low-flying birds were invited to listen, honor, and remember the life now passed.

Such solitary activities only catapulted me more deeply into matters of the unseen world. Was I developing an ever-keener sixth sense that had been with me all along? Was I a vessel for the inscrutable, a portal with the trust of a child?

I found comfort and solace in the book of Job:

> *If you would learn more, ask the cattle, Seek information from the birds of the air. The creeping things of earth will give you lessons, And the fishes of the sea will tell you all. There is not a single creature that does not know That everything is of God's making. God holds in power the soul of every living thing, And the breath of every human body.*
> —Book of Job 12:7–10 [1]

As the years passed, I was not satisfied to bask in private reverie. I wanted to understand the nature of these experiences, and I wanted to belong.

The Search for Understanding

I identified more with characters in Bible stories and Greek myths than everyday life activities with my peers. I longed to understand the deep instincts of those living in other times and places and despaired of the hollow life that surrounded me. What did Bushmen know that we have lost in the white noise of our artificially lit, harried lives? Is it possible that we have lost whole spiritual energies, ways to glimpse into the infinite realm that indigenous people have sustained? Is there a place for modern people to hear the music of the stars? Taste sound? Touch color? Is it possible that we have forgotten how to access glory, as our senses have grown dull, our deep instincts pruned? Are we so imprisoned by the soulless routines of daily life that have numbed our capacity to know vital spiritual energies of our inheritance?

Chances are, we all glimpse something deeper when we are awestruck with beauty, rest in stillness, or are transported into realms of love. In fact, is it possible that these abilities rest in the grooves of our neural circuitry?

It seems that many children sustain contact with the invisible world, often in play, a kind of "godly play" that British psychoanalyst W.D. Winnicott described in the life of the child. Childhood is a time in which a person lives especially close to his or her natural instincts, entertaining images and primal feelings of the unconscious life, before the risk of soul-crushing messages from family members, friends, teachers, playground bullies, and misguided authority figures force them underground. Some instincts are fed only by silence, easily drowned in the clanging of constant stimulation.

The soul hungers for the quietness of being and hibernates in the face of oversaturation.

For some, however, the soul will not be dissuaded, and the music of the spheres plays on to listening ears despite childhood wounds, daily assaults, and clamoring distractions. The sentient ones continue to hear the nightly stars.

These musings became my magnificent obsession, leading to five years in seminary and six years of graduate studies. The more I delved into my own psyche, examined the voices, received guidance, and lived with a quiet mind, the more confident I felt that this was my calling.

My simple childlike faith served its purpose—it got me through—but now I want to understand more about the invisible world, how it communicates, and to help others along the way. As a minister, a mother, a psychoanalyst, I envision the world as a paper screen that at any moment could grow thin or rip, exposing the singing stars waiting to perform for us, in full chorus.

A Glimpse Behind the Veil

CHAPTER 4

*There is a voice in the Universe urging us to re-
member our purpose for being on this great Earth.*
—Wayne Dryer

Much to my good fortune, this lonely period was short-
lived. When I was fourteen, I auditioned for an energetic
folk-singing group, The New Generation Singers, headed by a
Lutheran pastor fresh out of seminary who was not much more
than a teenager himself. Joining The New Generation Singers
opened the world of social justice to me during the erupting political climate of the 1960s.

Like many coming of age during this time, a political awakening was spreading across America, challenging the role of authority.
At the heat of this period, I lost my first boyfriend to the Vietnam
War. Dave was a working class kid who grew up in the church
singing gospel music and dazzling all of his with his beautiful tenor
voice. We had lots of wholesome fun with other church teens.
Nearly four years older than I was, he was my first kiss and opened
my heart in that early teenage love/crush that is like none other.

Drafted fresh out of high school, Dave was terrified of entering
the army. The night before he headed for Vietnam, Dave couldn't

locate the country on a world map or articulate why he was being sent there. In November of my junior year we learned of his death. The church's claim that "it must have been God's will" shook the foundation of my unquestioning theology.

Singing with the group channeled my grief and outrage, broke my bubble of loneliness, and provided a warm sense of belonging. I never wanted to feel weird again. I couldn't dismiss what I knew about the invisible realm but I longed to join in the secular world while fulfilling my call to the Good News of the Gospels. (It was a time of remembering and forgetting, remembering and forgetting again.) But when yet another message from the invisible world carried me to a foreign landscape, it was harder to forget for very long.

The Second Mystical Call

Though I still mourned for Dave, and felt outraged about the war, nearly two years had passed, and I had my jovial band of singer-friends, high school was behind me, and I anticipated a fun summer before heading off to college. Despite the continued backdrop of early loss, I was excited about so much that lay ahead.

It was in this mood on a warm June afternoon that a friend and I took a leisurely bike ride in rural Ohio. Having stopped in an open meadow to drink in this perfect summer day, we ambled back to our bicycles to head home. No sooner had I placed my hands on the handlebars to hop on my bike when suddenly my legs grew wobbly and collapsed beneath me. I lowered myself onto the warm gravel on the shoulder of the country road and felt my body drifting. I don't remember the next few minutes, although I do recall my mother arriving and my friend carrying me into the back seat of the old Buick. I carry a vague impression of my mother putting the bike in the trunk of the car as she anxiously drove back into town.

I woke under a cotton sheet on the living room couch, looking around the familiar room as if seeing everything for the first time. I heard my mother's voice as she spoke to our family doctor, asking if she should take me to the local emergency room. I caught my mother's eye and gave her a strained smile to assure her it was unnecessary; I was fine. Her eyes were flooded with fear as I silently held her gaze.

I must have again drifted off, for the next memory is that of traveling down a narrow tunnel toward a bright light. I saw what I perceived to be the figure of Jesus, offering an outstretched hand. I floated toward him and together we went to the edge of the tunnel. As far as I could see, angel-like creatures radiating shades of gold and white light were working in fields of deep amber. They were working the ground, moving their arms, appearing to be farmhands, hunched over and harvesting as far as I could see.

The images I saw in my mind's eye weren't unlike those in art books or in the halls of museums worldwide: the brilliant light, a hand outstretched, farmhands glorified in fields of gold. Did this iconography grace museum walls because artists, throughout time, have had similar visions; or do we have similar visions because we've absorbed the canon of art? All I can say is, mesmerized by the golden glow in a deafening silence, I was enveloped by boundless love while breathing in unspeakable peace and joy. This must be heaven, I thought. As I dissolved into the energy of this magnificent place, I mused, *how could anyone ever be afraid of dying?* In that moment, I knew there was nothing to fear, not now nor ever.

At that point, Jesus turned to me and asked if I'd like to come with him and together enter, or return back to my life on earth. I looked in the direction of his outreached hand and peered back toward the tunnel. I then had the sense of standing outside of my body; I could observe the teenage girl on the living room couch, my mother sitting nearby, and my young father's handsome face (having now arrived home from work), and wondered if they could handle losing a child.

When my eyes again met Jesus', he knew what I was thinking and offered reassurance, saying, "I know that you do not feel like you fit in, but if you choose to return, life will be different now. You are called to service. You will never be alone. You will always have the help you need." I looked down the Earth-bound tunnel and knew I needed to return. I began slowly walking away from Jesus and the brilliant light and floated into the narrow dark passageway. Gradually, I became aware of my physical breath and recognized my surroundings. I was back in our family living room.

In the hours that followed, I was physically exhausted and alternated between deep sleep and lightly dozing. I felt new and different. I had no understanding of the passing of time, and even now, I don't know if the few memories that have remained took place over several hours or days. I do recall struggling to stand with my mother's help but collapsing back on the couch. I remember struggling to speak. It felt as if I'd been drugged. I heard sounds of higher and lower frequencies than before. I marveled over household items in the living room. I saw with new eyes.

I gazed into our family terrier's deep brown eyes and realized that I hadn't really known Skippy Lou before, even though I had grown up with her. Now, I understood the meaning of her whimpering and intermittent barks. I heard her playful pawing and perceived her high-pitched whines to be gales of laughter. I was dumbstruck by Skippy's humorous assurance that she understood exactly what was happening.

In fact, Skippy Lou was helping me transition back to earth. It was as if I were asking the question posed by the Little Prince to the geographer, "What planet would you advise me to visit now?" To which he answered: "The planet Earth. It has a good reputation."

I dozed away, growing acclimated to my body and surroundings. Gradually, speech became easier with a natural cadence, movement returned easily, even as I felt like I was walking on air for several days. I passively reflected on a number of existential, religious, and personal questions: How long will it take to return to that same girl who was riding her bike, enjoying high school graduation? Who am I now? Will I remember my personality, now that I know I am *not* my personality? Will the concerns and interests of this world hold meaning for me now that I have seen heaven? Is this how Jesus felt when he descended to earth? Who else knows this? Will we recognize one another? Can we talk about this place? I had glimpsed a transcendent reality behind the soft veil that separates the worlds; everything was new.

From this point on, my sense of place in the larger cosmos was different. Although I was still uncertain as to what the actual call "to be of service" looked like, I was confident that my mission was to bring more light and love into the world.

It took years to understand what happened on that warm June afternoon. While I never doubted the reality of the experience, I didn't know its source or how to interpret it. I had never heard of near-death experiences, near-death-like experiences, altered states, peak experiences, or spiritual or transpersonal experiences. And if anyone did know about such experiences, they sure weren't talking with me in this conservative Ohio town.

What I did know were Old Testament stories in which God spoke to men of old, angels appeared and wrestled with mortals, and destinies were declared. These tales kept me afloat and gave me a context for self-understanding. But I longed to meet others who were called, who spoke with otherworldly creatures and delved into the mystery of their call. I counted on the reassurance of scripture, "Ask and it shall be given. Knock and the door will be open to you."

I was asking and knocking, and world religion scholar Huston Smith answered.

The first to attend college in my family, I soaked in the whole scene of Hiram College outside Cleveland: classes, discussions, meeting students from diverse backgrounds, and my own growing independence. But it was Huston Smith who pointed me in the right direction.

Smith was on a college lecture circuit from the Massachusetts Institute of Technology (MIT) speaking on world religions. Buzzing with infectious enthusiasm, Smith painted a religious worldview that embraced all traditions and sacred practices. The son of missionaries, Smith grew up in China and embraced the transcendent nature of all faiths with a perspective that invited the whole of humanity to unseen realms and personal freedom. I was stupefied by such heresy, fearful that the Lord would strike him dead at the podium; and, simultaneously, dazzled by the possibility that such a "wrong" could be a "right." How could someone support missionaries in India *and* Buddhist teachers in America? *How would anyone be saved if they believed in other faiths?* I wondered. I heard my father's voice warning that I would get confused when I attended Lutheran, Methodist, Baptist, Catholic, and Episcopal services in the same month. But Smith spoke of Hindus, Buddhist, Muslims, *and* Christians without reservation and with a voice of acceptance all at the same time—and he didn't seem the least confused, or scared of being a heretic. He referenced voices, visions, and ancient guiding stories with equal measure. I was carried by his gleeful, open smile and dancing eyes and I knew he was not of this world alone.

Perhaps it was pure projection or personal desperation, or maybe a nose for spiritual guidance, but after hearing Huston Smith, I did not feel alone in the world again. Huston handed me an invitation to a larger life, giving me permission to throw open the doors of my own experience and find freedom in differences. I literally skipped down the sidewalk as I left the lecture hall on that warm October afternoon. Years later, when Huston became my professor, friend, and mentor, preached at my ordination ceremony, and blessed my children, the threads of understanding he gave to me as a college student became solid cloth.

From that event in the autumn of my sophomore year of college, I began to claim the glory of the vast and mysterious sacred world while loosening the reins of the literal Biblical interpretations that keep God hostage in a small box shaped by Western culture. Increasingly, I began to understand the religious wounding that is created when Mystery is reduced to literalism and fertile symbols converted to stone.

I began to study Eastern and Western philosophy, practice yoga, and pay attention to the countless ways the invisible realm touched my daily life. With each discovery, I reclaimed the joy I knew in childhood when I bellowed in Sunday School, "deep and wide, deep and wide, there's a fountain flowing deep and wide ..." and waved my little girl arms side to side. A nascent understanding of the questions of my childhood began to take shape. I increasingly trusted that there were others who'd been called. Furthermore, I found a growing faith that I could live in this world while experiencing things not of this world. I came home to myself.

Eastern philosophy and spirituality were beginning to burst on the scene in certain circles around the country, especially in California. While these notions are common in today's frame of reference, they were seen as suspect and "far-out" in the 1960s and 70s. Although I wasn't yet speaking openly about my own experiences, I was able to read about others who were exploring mind-altering states and asking some of the same questions. It was a brilliant time to come of age as a mystical seeker.

Insight and the Altered State

Growing interest in states of consciousness was not limited to the fringes, but quickly moved into academic fields of study, building a bridge between Eastern and Western thought. Defining related terms and qualities made it possible for a nuanced dialogue and wider research to open up. Increasingly, the nature of consciousness and its many variations became a subject worth studying, which increased awareness in the larger society.

Altered states of consciousness, commonly referred to as transcendent or transpersonal experiences, are now documented as experiences in every culture and tradition. In fact, it is reasonable to assume that each individual experiences transpersonal moments at some point in his or her life span, even if it is not recognized as such. And furthermore, transcendent or transpersonal experiences influence our lives in significant ways.

The work of researcher P.M.H. Atwater suggests that ninety percent of all Nobel Prize winners base their life-changing work on sudden bursts of insight from dreams, images and visions that rise out of altered states. Everyday people in congregations around the world report transpersonal events to their pastors, priests, rabbis, and monks. The work of Atwater and Raymond Moody, among others, estimates 5% of the human population, which totals about 330 million, have reported near-death experiences, if only to a few trusted friends. An untold portion of the population believes that they have witnessed such strange unpredictable occurrences that they can only call them miracles. Nonetheless, as common as some of these experiences are, and increasingly acknowledged in recent years, there are many types of altered states of consciousness that are denied, minimized, or lived in silence and unnamed.

Like my own experience in childhood, many people across their life span live in fear of being misunderstood, perceived as strange, or labeled as downright crazy. Delving into the nature of those experiences, and specifically unpacking the mystical events, which summon assignments to a particular task or way of being, can help untold thousands of others to understand such altered states of consciousness, integrate them for their own growth, and transform them into ways that serve our world.

PART II

Naming the
Unnamable

CHAPTER 5

Nothing is harder yet nothing is more necessary,
than to speak of certain things whose existence is
neither demonstrable nor probable.
—*Hermann Hesse*, The Glass Bead Game

In my search to understand the essence of the mystical experience, it has been necessary to sift through a wide range of non-rational experiences. Increasingly understood as *transpersonal experiences*, or *TPEs* as I frequently refer to them, I began to categorize similarities and differences among varied states of consciousness and name the most defining qualities to distinguish one experience from the other, working my way to a more comprehensive grasp of the meaning of the mystical call.

Types of Transpersonal Experiences

There are many states of consciousness and types of transpersonal experiences, but for my purposes, I separate transpersonal experiences into six sub-categories: intuitive, psychic, paranormal, spiritual, religious, and mystical. Organizing the most common TPEs makes it easier to understand, distinguish, and discuss the experiences with increased specificity, even as many overlap and can be fully known only by the one experiencing them directly. Understandably, transpersonal experiences cannot be minimized or forced into any one box or definition. As psychiatrist Carl Jung taught, "Know your labels, but lay them aside when you deal with the beauty of the human soul."

Intuition

Of these six general subcategories of TPEs, intuitive experiences are the most common and easily recognized. In fact, they are so common in daily life that intuitive responses are normalized and easily forgotten except when they are punctuated by significant or determining life events. Some, of course, should be explained away as coincidence, but others are so clear as to be surely linked. Intuition is often experienced as a "gut feeling," literally setting off a chain reaction, from bodily discomfort to tingling sensations or goose bumps.

Such visceral knowing is universal to the human experience, tweaking our everyday choices and, potentially, even saving our lives. While traveling in Viet Nam, a pilgrimage to honor Dave, my boyfriend killed in the war, I met a quiet, big-hearted woman on her own healing pilgrimage. Returning to Saigon, now Ho Chi Minh City, she longed to understand the intuition that saved her life. A "gut feeling" guided her to float silently in the nearby river as enemy forces marched past. She continued to float for what seemed like a long time until an American serviceman, also hiding along the lush river bank, noticed that she was breathing, pulled her out of the water, and carried her to safety. She soon learned that her entire village along the river had been massacred. Her intuitive guidance saved her life.

How do we know what we know? What in our bodies pulls

us to broader insight, wisdom, and safety? Why do we sometimes follow it and other times deny or refuse its guidance? What signs may we have missed?

An extrasensory (or psychic) knowing, or an event of synchronicity, often accompanies intuitive experiences. It is only when carefully tracking one's own experiences in everyday life that one identifies the string of ESP aspects of intuition as the events occur. A possible example of quotidian fortune: While driving home from work recently, I remembered that we were running low on fruit and milk for breakfast. I momentarily wondered if I should take a different route and stop by the supermarket before going home. Tired, I thought of all the other food items in the house that I could serve for breakfast and continued driving. About a mile down the road, I had a strong feeling to return toward to the store, and at the last minute took the final exit off the Interstate. As I entered the store, I had an inclination to add freshly baked muffins and bagels, not my typical purchases. Nonetheless, I figured it would be a tasty surprise for the kids and headed home. Remaining on the back roads, I bypassed the Interstate.

Pulling into my driveway, I heard the announcer on the local radio station warn drivers of a traffic jam on the interstate due to a stalled vehicle. I had missed the pile-up as a result of running my errand. Without giving it much thought, I went in and unloaded the groceries on the kitchen island. My eyes drifted to a note my daughter left on the counter from her teacher requesting food donations of muffins and bagels for a special breakfast to honor the school's administrative staff tomorrow.

Seemingly insignificant, ordinary moments like these are common feelings that ribbon their way through everyday life circumstances, illustrating a synchronistic quality that confirms the intuitive hunch.

Extrasensory Perception

Psychic experiences, like intuitive ones, are also known through a "felt sense," which predicts a future moment (*i.e.*, identifying the caller before the phone is answered, or "feeling" someone is going to pass away before knowledge of the death is received). Psychic experiences, unlike intuitive ones, can occur not only in waking states, but also in trance, meditative, and dream states.

Such was the case when I dreamed that a cabin door of an airplane suddenly opened while flying from over the Pacific Ocean. I awoke in a panic and "knew" that despite my willingness to interpret the dream within the context of my own personal life factors, the dream was a premonition. Distressed as to when or how the incident might occur, I contacted several close family members and friends and warned them about an impending disaster.

I maintain a dream journal, and even today I can revisit the entry for Feb. 22, 1989. I wrote, *I see individuals being sucked out of a plane. I tried to count the bodies, but it was nearly impossible, both because of my own panic that I was feeling in the dream and the power of the atmosphere and moving parts. I believe there were 6 people sucked out, but it could have been 7, 8, or 9. Somehow a door had opened and these poor people were sucked out. Although I was uncertain of the origins of the flight, I could see Honolulu in the distance. I awoke knowing it was a premonition and I was shaking and horrified. Will this occur in a few days, weeks or months? I don't know. I just want to pray for those who lost their lives and their families as they live through this. I am guessing it will happen soon.*

On February 24, the extremely disturbing situation came to pass. It was a United Airlines flight from Honolulu to Sydney in which there was a cargo door failure resulting in the loss of lives in a situation of unbearable terror. I was grief stricken for the passengers and their loved ones. It is not the sort of premonition anybody would wish to have.

Paranormal Experiences

Paranormal experiences, another type of TPE, are commonly identified as seeing ghosts, flying objects, extraterrestrial, or otherwise invisible entities. This experience usually involves an encounter with a being or entity from another realm and forever shapes one's worldview and belief in the existence of an unseen reality. Understandably, reactions of awe and terror are common. Like other transpersonal experiences, one's self-perception as well as one's understanding of reality and other dimensions is altered.

Ghost, or haunted-house, stories are a part of our culture, but generally are not taken seriously by many in mainstream culture. They are typically less common than ESP experiences and more threatening since they propose an energy dimension that is less understood.

Such was the case for my family when we participated in a house-exchange in the desert of southern California on a popular home-exchange website. Contacted by a party interested in visiting Florida, my two teens and I agreed to the exchange, and brought along one of their friends, anticipating a restful holiday with time to explore the desert and see the sites of Los Angeles within driving distance.

I can't say that I had any particular intuitive feeling about the anticipated vacation or the initial entry into the home. On the first morning after our evening arrival, however, I recall a tingling sensation while sitting at the breakfast table. Arising early to work on a mental-health treatment program for crime victims, I became aware of an eerie unfamiliar sensation. I initially dismissed it, believing that it was a natural, sensitive response to some of the upsetting cases I was reviewing, on an early quiet morning in an unfamiliar home. I didn't give it much thought until several inexplicable events began to occur over the next couple days.

The first, we tried to explain away numerous times: The unloaded dishwasher spontaneously began running, despite the knob set to the off position. I imagined that the dishwasher was on an automatic timer that I couldn't locate, so I overlooked it. I also ignored the lights going on and off. After all, houses have their own unique features and electrical settings. Even when the outside glass door began rattling without provocation, I imagined that low-flying planes bound to a nearby airfield must be causing the door to vibrate. Or an earthquake? And when I walked outside to the stone silent desert landscape, I turned my attention to the teenagers, believing that one of the kids must have been out by the pool and, finding the back door locked, made her way around to the front, first giving the knob a firm shake.

Calling out to each girl, I ascertained that everyone was reading or watching movies upstairs, and returned to my perch in the dining room to continue reading. Within moments, the same thing happened again. This time, I watched the glass vibrate and the knob turn in front of me. Now I was the one rattled. I called out, asking if someone would google the owner's name posted on the front of the home. It was time to figure out what was happening, or contact the owner.

Galloping down the stairs, the eyes of my daughter's friend doubled in size as she breathlessly handed me her cell phone. I scanned the *L.A. Times'* report: a murdered girl, her youthful beauty smiling from the chilling article—and now, from the nearby photo on the wall beside me. It had been a huge local story at the time, a double murder that at this time was hanging in the courts, with those arrested suspended in jail, and a family and community devastated. I soon discovered that the house, built as a "Mommy and Me" project, was the beautiful teenage girl's home; her bedroom, despite its water view, unchosen in the selection of bedrooms.

Gathering everyone together, we headed into town for a pizza to get some needed space from the house and discuss what was happening. Together, we reviewed the tragedy of the murder, and one-by-one each girl confessed minor yet inexplicable happenings. All had refrained from sharing their observations for fear of spooking out anyone else. None of us had ever experienced a paranormal event, but we all began to calm ourselves and breathe more deeply as we acknowledged and named what we had each privately thought.

When we returned to the house, the dishwasher again greeted us. This time, our friend called out the deceased girl's name and commanded, "Please stop it." Immediately, the dishwasher moaned to a grinding halt and clicked off. We shivered but oddly felt better, as if we had some control. It never occurred again during our visit, although a glass of water left on my night table was now on the wood floor at the foot of my bed.

While I have never before or since recognized this kind of paranormal activity, I have increased awareness and sensitivity for veterans of such experiences who feel frightened, even traumatized, by such unseen entities.

Like foretelling intuitive and ESP experiences, paranormal events are multi-layered and overlap in the defining characteristics of other TPEs. They typically carry specific messages, although they are not easily deciphered by the rational mind. This is the case with Joy-Lynne, who later became a friend. While working in her Frederick, Maryland, mountain art studio, she created, as she explains in an interview, *"an exact drawing of my personal spiritual guide that came to me in a trance-like creative state."* This was a face unfamiliar to her, but when she finished the drawing, she knew that she was destined to be in a relationship with the person in this image. Previously, she had experienced him only as a spirit guide in her mind who offered advice and counsel. But now, after the drawing, she believed that he existed and that, somehow, their paths would cross.

Joy-Lynne's drawing fits into several transpersonal categories:

First, it was an intuitive experience in that she had a gut feeling to draw a particular figure. Second, it held an ESP event in that she knew that she would later recognize the presence shown in the drawing and that she was meant to be in a relationship with him in actual waking life. And finally, it was a paranormal event in that it included a *spirit*, who arrived and guided her from another plane of reality as she drew.

Years later, she met and married a man who precisely matched the image of her spirit guide. Did she subconsciously seek someone who resembled the image? Maybe, but that's no less spiritual: Whether the figure guided her, or she guided herself, an enigmatic path led to clarity and fulfillment.

Spiritual Experiences

While many people balk at the term *spiritual*, sometimes it is the most fitting word to capture an extraordinary state of awe and wonder. Many spiritual states occur while in nature, such as floating on a vast body of warm water or staring at the heavens on a clear starry night. Other awestruck moments are achieved while making love, lost in a deep creative state, or while sitting bedside with a dying relative or friend. Still others describe a spiritual experience when they, themselves, are preparing for death.

Spiritual TPEs are recognized by the feelings of openness, expansion and connection to the larger world community or cosmos. There is often a resounding peace during and immediately following the experience. Furthermore, spiritual transpersonal experiences transcend any one particular faith or religious belief system or deity, and are among the most accessible and publicly accepted TPEs, a gateway perhaps to deeper states. They touch the heart— and in an instant, weave an ever-widening web of connection to the entire planet.

Religious Experiences

A religious transpersonal experience occurs within the context of a particular faith tradition or inspires one toward that specific tradition. This kind of TPE usually serves to validate a specific religious orientation and deepens one's faith. For others, it is a transpersonal experience that precedes conversion to a specific faith or creed. For example, when I would pray as a child and slip into audible ramblings of a language that I didn't understand, often trembling and staring into space, I experienced what I now know as ecstasy. I was in communion with The Other in a transcendent reality. Free of place and time, I felt transported into a state of rapture. I believed that I was in communion with God, as I understood him from the teachings of the evangelical Pentecostal Assembly of God church. This transpersonal experience was deeply spiritual in that I felt connected to a larger world, but the experience was first and foremost an experience that I interpreted as a confirmation of the Christian faith.

Religious and spiritual transpersonal experiences are similar but differ in the cognitive and emotional aftereffects. Typically, purely spiritual experiences expand one's emotional response to include the whole of humanity, while the religious experience supports a bond with others, but primarily strengthens one's faith in one particular tradition and religious figure.

Mystical Experiences

The mystical experience may overlap with other transpersonal experiences, but it is distinct in that there is an encounter with another entity, deity, or symbol that may or may not be a recognizable religious figure. The experience opens gateways to transcendent understanding and transports the individual to a numinous realm.

This experience is an encounter, one that is described by poets, sages and saints throughout history that leaves one awestruck and terrified at the same time. Absorbed into this Sacred Other, the veil to a larger mystery is temporarily lifted and forever changes one's sense of reality. Defying description, the mystical experience is ineffable, beyond language. In theological terms, there is a *quickening* that occurs in Spirit. The common aftereffects are awe and rapture for hours or even days afterwards.

When certain charismatic Christian groups participate in speaking in tongues or prophesy as channeled through a God encounter, one may claim that some individuals are experiencing a mystical event. Like all mystical experiences, it cannot be intellectually comprehended in normal waking consciousness.

Mystical Calls

The mystical call is a specific kind of mystical experience in that it not only includes an encounter with the *other* but also carries a message, which informs its recipient of his or her destiny. The call deepens in meaning and offers guidance throughout the recipient's life span.

The differences between the spiritual, religious, and mystical experiences were highlighted while I was visiting a convent of aging nuns in rural south England, dating from 1901. It was a lovely part of Berkshire, in a town called Ascot. One elderly sister described her sunrise walks through a nearby garden in which she meditates on an image of her heart holding a burning candle that had come to her as a young schoolgirl. For Sister Joan, the lit candle is a reminder to carry light in her heart as she engages with a dark and broken world. As she strolls through the dew-covered grass, she describes a sensation of her heart opening with compassion for the whole world and feels at peace. This morning ritual prepares her to love others as she begins her day, a *spiritual* inspiration.

Another nun, Sister Agnes, described a time when Mother Mary, the Mother of God, came to her late at night while saying the rosary. Sister Agnes grew increasingly disoriented, not knowing where Mary ended and she began. Blinded by Mary's piercing light, she could not see what was happening, but she knew that Mary was blessing her hands as she held her rosary. The nun's hands became Mary's hands as the rosary glided through their fingers. This left her feeling in a state of reverie, filled with love for everyone around her and confident that she had made the right choice when she converted to Catholicism and entered the convent. It gave her confirmation, through a *mystical* experience.

One day, Mother Bernadette spoke to me of a light-infused male figure that approached her while she walked along the levee on a summer evening. Speechless, she fell to her knees in ecstasy on the soft summer grass and lost all sense of time and place. The earth spun as she lay listening to a voice coming through the visiting figure. In hushed tones, he instructed her to start an orphanage for the low-caste abandoned babies in rural southern India. This *mystical call* shaped the course of her life.

Learning to decipher and name the different types of experiences provides a framework to understand the distinction between a religious or spiritual experience, a mystical experience, and a mystical call. Each experience carries its own meaning and power, but given that the mystical call is marked with a life assignment, it serves as a revelatory labyrinth to fulfill one's individual destiny.

In Search of
Mystical Calls

CHAPTER 6

The most beautiful emotion we can experience is the mystical. It is the power of all true art and science. He to whom this emotion is a stranger, who can no longer wonder and stand rapt in awe, is as good as dead. To know that which is impenetrable to us really exists, manifesting itself as the highest wisdom and most radiant beauty, which our dull faculties can comprehend only in their most primitive forms—this knowledge, this feeling, is at the center of true religiousness. In this sense, and in this sense only, I belong to the rank of devoutly religious men.

—Albert Einstein

Living the Questions

I grew to understand the poet Rilke's advice to "live the questions" in deciphering the different types of transpersonal experiences and developing an ear for mystical calls. Heartened with hundreds of stories gathered in my search to understand the meaning of mystical calls, I learned a deeper whole-body listening, becoming swept into my own assignment: to help others understand and fulfill their calls. But first, I had to be willing to wait, to sacrifice the ego's rush for certainty.

During this period, I anchored myself in my own Judeo-Christian roots and reviewed the stories of my childhood. The same qualities that define mystical calls from antiquity show themselves in the Judeo-Christian tradition. The Old Testament provides stories of individuals called from a variety of settings and for different purposes. Most often, individuals were called to instruct others as to God's will and, in so doing, bring people into the right relationship. Some were prepared and eager to receive God's instruction, as illustrated in the well-known scripture of Isaiah: "I saw the Lord sitting upon a throne, ... and his train filled the temple ... I heard the voice of the Lord saying, whom shall we send?" Then I said, "Here am I, send me" (Isaiah 6:1–8).

The prophet Ezekiel had a vision in which the heavens opened and he was filled with a divine spirit that remained in him (Ezekiel 2:1–2). Jeremiah (Jeremiah 2:2) and Samuel (Samuel 3:11–12) heard God's voice directly and responded. Moses (Exodus 31:1–17) and Gideon received callings through the Angels of God. Other accounts in the Old Testament depict resistance to God's call as in the story of Jonah. Instructed to go to Nineveh, Jonah attempted to escape God's order and followed the demand only after being swallowed in the belly of a whale (Jonah 1:2–15).

In the New Testament, the assignments began to include instructions as to new ways of living. Individuals were called to assume certain qualities and characteristics. Callings were specified as salvation, holiness, and faith (2 Thessalonians 2:13f.) Other calls included the goals of fellowship (1 Corinthians 1:9), service (Galatians 1), and eternal life (Hebrews 9:15). The dominant New Testament theme was God's call to convert to a new system of values through the acceptance of Jesus as the Messiah and to preach the gospel. The story of Saul's vision that characterized his conversion to Christianity and to preach the good news is a predominant example of a New Testament mystical call.

Certainly, the life of Jesus can be categorized as the call of the shaman and healer who participated in the universal themes of sacrifice, death, and rebirth to bring the wisdom of a new Adam into human evolution. We see the suffering in his solitude in the Garden of Gethsemane in preparation for his crucifixion and the reported resurrection to save the world. These Biblical reports incorporate powerful initiatory rites from pre-historic universal traditions. It is the archetypal story of the wounded healer.

Other examples of early mystical calls documented by scholar Mircea Eliade include a mystical encounter of the Iranian Zarathustra (Zoroastrian) in the first millennium BC who claimed to be called by his God, Ahura Mazda. Zarathustra was instructed to preach God's impending reign. Another is the prophet, Mani (b. 216 AD), founder of Manichaeism, whose mystical experience called him to preach salvation to his people.

The examples are numerous. As I worked my way back through history, I discovered extensive documentation of mystical calls before organized religion moved onto the world stage. Nor are mystical calls restricted to primitive medicine men with snake spirits, but continue over time across all bodies of knowledge and vocations. Sometimes the mystical call is historically identified by a totem or symbol, as is the case of the snake emblem, the Serpent of Epidaurus, which refers back to the tutelary patron of physicians, Aesculapius, who followed his call. Greek history points to the private voice heard and followed by Socrates. In literature, we hear the call in Goethe's famous opus, *Faust*.

In modern history, mystical calls are illustrated in private diaries pointing individuals in life-determining directions. Such is the case of Telesphoros, who is said to have dictated his inspired medical prescriptions from a voice that guided him from another sphere. In some records, mystical calls refer to the voice of the daemon - known in Greek mythology as a supernatural being who serves as an intermediate between the gods and human beings that summons one in a direction that had to be followed against all odds.

Edging more and more deeply into religious history with my dog-eared, story-filled index cards in hand, I knew that I was face-to-face with some of the most significant spiritual phenomena in the history of humanity, one that extends throughout the centuries to the present moment. Present-day stories were linking arms with a deeper ancestral heritage.

I listened carefully to each story that carried a sacred tailwind. Stories from friends, neighbors, and strangers at bus stops, on the train or in the coffee shop, fueled by a divine energy, reeled me in. I filled my diary with observations, sketched existing patterns, compared and contrasted the similar and different characteristics of any reference to calls.

Increasingly, I heard the term *calling* used in secular contexts removed from its historical roots in religion, art, mythology and anthropology. The term has now been adopted in contemporary parlance as it surfaced from the field of career counseling, referring to a strong urge, deep instinctive hunch, or a niggling intuitive impulse. While the secular usage of the word has its own unique power and meaning, the original word is from mythology and religious history and carries distinct qualities, patterns, and life trajectories that touch the mystical.

To know this distinction, I waited patiently for that rare call that is characterized by the mystics of old: it was otherworldly. Time passed as I held on to my handwritten, yellowing notecards. I waited and listened, preparing myself for the next story to appear, and like manna from above, in due time, the stories arrived. Some came with an effortless blast of energy, while some were shared with pressured speech in fits and starts. Some were disclosed only after the gentlest of coaxing. Nearly every experience was recounted in hushed tones—even if the voice was animated, as if a long-held secret were about to be spilled at long last. Each speaker tested for personal safety, guarding the sanctity of every vision seen and voice heard. As I tracked each unique mystical story, there were identifiable, repeated themes, patterns, and characteristics. A longed-for mystical map was revealing itself.

And as grace would show itself, it was during this time that I found the extraordinary work of mythologist Joseph Campbell. Campbell's scholarship and passion for ancient myths breathed a fresh appreciation for mythology and story into Western consciousness. Campbell's work, along with that of William James and Evelyn Underhill, offered broad supportive shoulders as I traveled through mystical history.

My days of feeling isolated became a distant memory. I had found my tribe, both historically and currently. All the while, shared stories were few and far between, and reluctant. Fear of being misunderstood or seen as sick or "weird" (the root of which derives from the Old English meaning fate or destiny) is still common. I heard some stories shared for the first time, with eruptions of personal catharsis after years of hiding the experience. For others, there was a reckoning in acknowledging the determining power the mystical call had held in their lives. And as I claimed the meaning of my own experiences, I grew to inhabit my vulnerability and find an intimacy with it that opened my heart and, paradoxically, increased my objectivity as I entered into this untraveled space.

Patterns and Themes Emerge

Increasingly, the shared patterns, qualities, and themes of all mystical calls—regardless of time, place, religion, and culture—became apparent. For example, most mystical calls occur in early life. I was not quite four when I heard the voice of the angel protecting my family. I was ten when I was told to serve the Gospels. I had just turned eighteen when I traveled to another realm and was instructed to give my life to service. While calls can occur at any age, many calls take place in early life.

Is this because the child is more open and available to the unseen world? Is there an inherent spiritual receptivity of the universal child and hence, the call is received? Some traditions believe that a child's consciousness is more open to the spiritual realm before he or she adapts to the material world and the personality is shaped by repression and compensation. Perhaps a star of destiny touches us all, but we soon forget, trading in the sacred consciousness for survival and approval as the pressures of the physical world move in.

In time, the calls found me. They spanned the globe: from fast-paced urban lifestyles of Manhattan and Hong Kong to small towns in Scotland and rural villages in Indonesia. With every story in each unique setting, a shared theme marked the experience: the mystical call was fed by a living archetypal stream of consciousness that erupted in the individual and opened a spiritual portal that could now be identified and, increasingly, understood.

Mystical Calls as Initiations

CHAPTER 7

Like stars over dark fields, love is the gift of the eternal forces. We do not know why it appears: it is just the song the universe sings to itself. And, like other beauties, it is a demanding guest. As soon as love arrives, we have to serve it—we were naked and now must put on clothes and work.   —John Tarrant

As I continued to immerse myself in the rich history and personal narratives of those who have experienced a mystical call, I recognized that the mystical call served as an initiation into a larger life, a life that transcended time and place; a life that beckoned to a path that was no longer of one's own making. I also recognized that each story, regardless of time, place, age, religion, culture, or gender shared certain archetypal themes with every other called individual.

A Precipitating Event

Those who report a mystical call share a wide range of experiences with every other mystical call. Not only do a high percentage of calls occur in childhood as previously referenced, but throughout the history of mystical calls, a precipitating event, or what may be called an initiatory crisis, can occur before the actual call takes place. For some, it is a tragic set of life circumstances such as an illness, accident, or inexplicable loss of consciousness. For others, the initiatory crisis is a psychological trauma, the loss of a family member, job, or unexpected abandonment by a spouse. Others survive a natural disaster, including earthquakes, snowstorms, forest fires, and hurricanes, as happened to Rachel prior to being called.

As Rachel sat huddled in a small closet, praying that she would survive Hurricane Marilyn, the closet door suddenly blew off, exposing the whirling cloud-banked sky. Where once had been a sliding glass door, she could see the homes and buildings in the distance dangling on the hillside of St. Thomas. The roof continued to collapse, which gave way to windows crashing to the ground, opening a perfect view of motorcycles and large appliances bouncing down the hillside. Everyday household items were now torpedoes driven into the trembling ground with each fresh gust of racing wind.

When the wind and rain finally subsided, Rachael crawled out across the collapsed roof that now carpeted her living room and climbed over toppled furniture and shattered debris to an open space. Finding a clear space to stand, she noticed the built-in bookcase unmoved. While every book and item on the shelf was now strewn amidst the rubble, one item remained: her grandmother's menorah. She picked it up. Uncertain if she had lost consciousness or was merely disoriented from the terror, Rachel felt the weight of the menorah melt into her body as she shook her head, muttering,

"Yes, yes, yes." Propping herself up on the collapsed roof, she heard the call to become a rabbi and recognized her place in life is, in her words, "with the Jewish people."

Others, like Karl, endured not a natural crisis, but a psychological one. Karl received the call in stillness, even deafening silence, like the one I heard during the summer camp vesper service. In his early forties, Karl was married and a father, a successful professor in New York City, with an apartment in Manhattan and a farmhouse upstate. Despite these noted accomplishments, Karl was often unhappy and, at times, drinking heavily. He refers to this time as one of "psychological despair." It was in this state that Karl experienced a call that changed his life.

During the spring of 1992, while he was teaching a graduate course, a student gave a presentation on St. Teresa of Avila and described her personal visit to a monastery. During the student's presentation, Karl knew something profound was stirring inside. It was piercing through his depression and Monday morning haze. In hindsight, he linked this with the events of the following weekend. While fixing up his old upstate farmhouse the Saturday after the student's presentation, he awoke in the middle of the night with the clear, unmistakable knowledge that there was something invisible in the room. Although he had never experienced anything like this before, he knew he was being visited by a spiritual presence. He turned to look toward the small wooden bedroom door and then slowly around the room, but nothing was there.

As he explains it, "utter peace and tranquility came over me and I was cradled in the arms of a soft light. I recall asking, *What do you want from me?* but all I can remember is melting into the presence. I don't know how much time passed or what happened next. I felt light, a loss of gravity, and a stillness that is unspeakable. I was alone in the middle of the night in a context of virtual sensory deprivation. The silence and weightlessness transported me to an angelic realm and through an encounter with an angel, my life changed. I converted from a committed atheist to a man who was willing to surrender to a spiritual reality that governs the cosmos. I now understand that when everything else is taken away, there is a place that is not of this world. I was visited by an angel, and the encounter called me to change my life, not only in small everyday habits, but in the very foundation of my being."

Out of stillness or in a flurry of activity, prefaced by illness, stress, or accident, the otherworldly being, deity, symbol, or energy presents itself—and a call is voiced. The instructions may be specific, boasting elaborate detail, or a general assignment.

In my own story, I had an inexplicable fainting spell, followed by a loss of consciousness. I have now heard many stories of fainting right before the call. Researcher P.M.H. Atwater refers to such experiences as a "near death-like experience," which shares the qualities of the more commonly understood near-death phenomenon without a medical emergency or real threat of physical death. I was not overheated, nor did I have any medical condition, but without forewarning, I fainted. I had never fainted before and was not under distress in my young life. Nor had I ever had a seizure, hallucinated, or used drugs. Yet my experience was not unique among those who'd had mystical experiences.

Across the board, no one believed that he or she could have predicted such an experience to occur. Rather, a spontaneous mystical event erupted out of the blue. Despite the fact that some spiritual seekers long for intense transcendent encounters—and participate in various religious and esoteric practices to bring about such experiences—the genuine mystical experience is rarely one that can be manufactured on-demand. In fact, in my experience, not one reported that he or she had sought such an experience, although some longed for a deeper spiritual understanding in general.

The Physical and Emotional Nature of the Mystical Call

Not only is the authentic mystical call a spontaneous unplanned event, it is typically identified as one of the most—if not *the* most— powerful experiences known emotionally, physically, and spiritually. Only in hindsight are certain precursors identified prior to the experience, but the most remarkable markers are what happen during and after the mystical call. There is typically a specific identifiable physical reaction during and after the mystical encounter. Commonly, one's sense of physical weight is temporarily altered. Some feel light, defying all sense of gravity, as if floating through space. Others claim that they feel strangely heavy, so much so that they feel paralyzed, unable to move, a kind of catalepsy. Other common physical symptoms include a pounding heart and shortness of breath. Some individuals described an inability to "catch their breath" as if the wind was knocked out of them. Many describe a tingling or shaky sensation; others speak of uncontrollable trembling or vibrating.

Kylie described her mystical encounter as a physical explosion that she felt throughout her entire body: "I felt as if I was sitting before an atomic bomb and was blown away. It took everything in me to hold on to a physical reality and stay conscious given the enormity of the experience."

John reported that his senses were heightened and his heart was pounding so fiercely that he wondered if he were going to have a heart attack: "Not only was the pounding a terrifying experience, it was as if a million pounds were pressing on my chest. I couldn't move or help myself. I had the sensation that my heart was holding the weight of the world and I didn't know if I could stay alive with that much suffering in my body. Then, suddenly, the suffering became an expansive feeling of compassion for the whole world. I wondered if my heart would burst from the love of it all.

I could hardly breathe but tried to remain conscious. I have never felt anything like it before or since. The love was extraordinary. Afterwards, I couldn't move for a long time. When I finally stood up, I stared at the sky, and lost myself in the beauty of the night. Time evaporated."

Some people have a more acute awareness and memory of their physical sensations than others. Some quickly lost contact with their bodies as they drifted into a kind of trance state. Be it trembling, hyper-arousal, deafening stillness, pounding heart, or feeling punched in the gut, everyone reported strong physical reactions to a Presence that called them to change in character, belief, task, or life orientation.

The call itself is typically heard by a voice or seen in a vision—however, some 'hear' the call through a felt sensation. When there is no recognizable speech or vision, the individual simply "knows" through a multi-sensory message transmitted and understands the meaning of the message.

Some mystical calls are commonly felt as a kind of merging, as if all physical boundaries are released as they melt into The Other. Some individuals are absorbed into a particular sound, music, or chant and become transported to another realm in which the specific call is communicated. Others merge with the visual image and simply feel the instructions offered.

Following the experience, some people are disoriented for a period of time. The impact of the intensity and mind-blowing nature of the experience, along with the shock and fear of the tremendous responsibility of the actual assignment, leaves many people confused or even physically weak for several days. The most common time frame documented is a three-day period before people are fully reoriented physically, and even longer to process what actually happened—let alone begin to respond to the assignment itself.

In reviewing hundreds of calls, I now believe that the physical reaction may be the inability to maintain consciousness in the presence of the energy moving through one's body. In my experience, the energy of this encounter was more than my physical body could tolerate and as a result, I fainted and was left exhausted and disoriented for several days before returning to normal waking awareness.

Sri Nisargadatta Maharaj, a master in the Tantri Nath lineage, wrote in *The Nectar of Immortality,* "The merging of beingness within itself is the very fount of bliss. Many sages who are in such a state are quite oblivious to their physical condition and simply lie on the ground, reveling ..."

Given this universal three-day convalescence, one can speculate that this time frame and the number "three" holds meaning that is not coincidental. Though other numbers have mythological symbolism, *three* does seem unusually frequent in stories, myths, legends, formulas and teachings throughout history. Within world religions, Jesus rose from the dead on the third day; the Christian Trinity of Father, Son, and Holy Spirit; the Hindu ancient trinity of Brahma the Creator, Vishnu the Preserver, and Shiva the Destroyer; and in many areas in the East and elsewhere, the dead are typically left for three days before burial or burning.

Outside of religion, we humans are understood to have three distinct brain functions, often referenced as the Triune Brain: the reptilian, the limbic, and the neocortical. Geometrically, the three-sided triangle is believed to be the strongest, most powerful physical form known. Symbolically, the number three resonates with the archetypal energy Aditi who prepares the conscious mind to flow into the unconscious and surface with new symbols for self-growth. Perhaps there is a relationship between this prime number following a mystical call and a larger ancestral meaning that is yet to be understood.

The Call and the Community

Another shared characteristic among those who are called is that which begins as a singular personal experience grows into a communal one. Historically, mystical calls not only shape the individual life, they serve to initiate the *community* as well, summoning the tribe, clan, congregation, and society to greater wholeness and awareness beyond the individual messenger's personal desires, needs, or satisfaction. Even today, in our differentiated society and highly individualistic orientation, mystical calls can be identified as having a significant impact on the larger community.

Throughout history, communal stories reveal the call's shaping of the larger community. In tribal days and into modern religious circles, the community recognizes that there is a supernatural being or energy at play that has appointed one of their own—and, in kind, blessed their tribe or congregation. This becomes a source of celebration as well as a heightened sense of responsibility and accountability within the community.

While the community is typically elated at the upsurge in power and consciousness that the called individual will now offer the tribe, the individual selected may be undergoing a very complex and dark rite of passage. The called individual is commonly transitioning from the impact of the physical call itself and left to wrestle with the weight of the actual assignment, a kind of "facing off" with the gods. The mystical call becomes a rite of initiation to a Higher Allegiance, as referenced by mystical scholar Evelyn Underhill. In this regard, one's previously held identity and life goals are surrendered in exchange for a higher purpose. This purpose incorporates the ego while transcending it, in dedication to the work of the soul. Now, one envisions and dreams on behalf of the whole creation; no lightweight responsibility.

Recognizing that the larger community will be blessed in

having one who is called among them as a healer or leader, rituals and pageantry unique to the group are typically planned. While this is less common in contemporary society (with the exception of ceremonies in particular groups, including the military, political oaths, some clubs, and religious installations and ordinations), there is reason to believe that many current rituals and pageants have grown out of early ancient rites of passage. Some of the most elaborate early examples of celebratory rituals are seen in the Yuin, Wiradjure, and Kamilaroi tribes in Queensland, Australia, but such rites can be traced around the world. While the initiated healer, teacher, artist, or shaman holds a central place in the celebration, the entire community participates in activities that may go on for days or months. For participants, there is a heightened religious reverie, consistent with the anthropological notion of *participation mystique,* a term for the mysterious feeling of participating in the action of a drama, pageantry, ritual, or sporting event that enhances the consciousness of the larger group.

Some cultures also dramatize the initiation stages along with the final celebratory pageantry. Rites of passage from birth to awakening, suffering, the act of being called, sacrificial acts, and death of the secular self and resurrection to the new life are commonly acted out before the community. Such stages of initiation can be identified within many traditions, the most noted Western one being the events that led up to the Easter celebration in the Christian story. The message of surrender and sacrifice marks every major tradition, however. It is not only a dying to an outdated consciousness that must now be surrendered; it is an acceptance that new life and transformation do not live in separation but in relationship.

Recognized by the larger clan, one is now initiated into a new identity, given a new name, and manifests special gifts or abilities among the group. The call becomes one's true vocation, as captured in the Latin word *vocare,* meaning "to call, summon, or name."

From this voice, the true personality beyond the false identity of the ego is set in motion in allegiance to the Higher Self/Soul and carries the larger community into advanced consciousness. The ancient Persian poet Saadi may describe those who gather in purposeful community a kind of tribe: "This is a caravan, filled with eccentric beings telling wondrous stories about God."

Yes

CHAPTER 8

After the last no there is a yes, upon which the future world depends.   —Wallace Stevens

As the intensity of the call itself is absorbed and integrated into the psyche and physiology of the individual, there is a natural re-orienting process that occurs. Each person has his or her own pace and rhythm, and the experience provides a marker in time, a frame of reference in which life before and after the experience is forever demarcated.

Initially, the assignment itself may be overshadowed by the power of the felt experience. However, as one's physiology settles and the message is sorted out in conscious thought, one is then challenged to face what has been assigned; essentially, a call to face one's destiny of the True Self.

Finding the Yes

This ability to face one's destiny marks the beginning of the journey and punctuates the words of philosopher Gregory Vlastos with which I have chosen to open this book: "There are a thousand ways to say no, one way to say yes and no way of saying anything else. It is a tremendous decision."

An experience of the "yesness" as described by the late Episcopal priest Martin Bell begins from the moment in which we have a God-encounter and life is forever altered. Reality as previously known is snatched away given how such an encounter "shoves human beings up against the stark realties of finitude and unmitigated limitation ... But if we die to the world, cast our idols to the ground, and turn to the Giver of life, we shall find ourselves suddenly and unaccountably free. Those ... who have experienced the awesome, crushing, liberating hand of God, in the wake of that experience, have said Yes to reality ... real people, living real lives, buffeted by the headwind of God."

It is then this arduous process toward the "yes," that constitutes the development of the Self, a summons to *individuation*, a term used by Jung to describe actualizing the real self. Heeding the call as played out within each individual's personality structure, style, type, and defenses as well as the particular life circumstances, makes for the hard work of the call. This is the hero's journey according to mythologist Joseph Campbell. Here, each individual must face off with the personal beliefs and attitudes of the adapted small self of the ego to the higher allegiance of the Higher or True Self in order to fulfill the call, even as the attitude and role of the ego state must be respected. A changed attitude and relationship with the ego develops.

Mythologist Joseph Campbell describes this as the hero's journey, which always begins with a call: "'Look, you're in Sleepy Land. Wake. Come on a trip. There is a whole aspect of your consciousness, your being, that's not been touched. So you're at home here? Well, there's not enough of you here.' And so it starts."

For many, like myself, who received a call in early life, the self was largely unformed but shaped by a passionate desire to be a good steward. Wrestling with the complexes and defenses within oneself was unfamiliar and carried no frame of reference. Nor could I appreciate the hard theological work that was waiting. The small god of my evangelical church home was a valued place to begin the journey, but was an immature place to stay. To a great degree, one's God image is a reflection of the size of one's own understanding and heart. My childhood God grew out of a constricted communal heart; a religious subculture that was narrow, although well intentioned. Religiously and personally, the young self of the girl-child had little understanding of what was ahead, but fortunately, little was set in stone at that tender age. One must find one's God that fits into one's true "heart culture" as referenced by psychotherapist Marilyn Jenai.

Coming to terms with the "yes" is a different journey for those called in adulthood. It is often a more complicated passage when one's identity, beliefs, and relationship expectations are more set. Essentially, the ego structure and identity are more or less formed and defenses, attitudes, and choices that accompany development are in place. Arriving to the "yes" may entail a restless holy longing that will not be quieted or even a crushing blow to the ego to secure one's attention. As a result, there is pressure that forces change lest the soul is weakened through abandonment of the real self. Still, there may be loss and suffering as the individual is forced to face his or her own summons. Philosopher Alan Watts maintains that the true self is found when the false one is renounced.

Many choice-points leap on the horizon immediately following a mystical call. Each decision provides the nutrients to birth and strengthens the "yes," as one travels this great labyrinthine way. For some, the initial weeks and months following a mystical call may include episodes of solitude, alienation, loneliness, disorientation, and self-doubt. Simultaneously, there appears to be invisible assistance and reassurance at play. My vision of Jesus promised assistance, and others commonly report enigmatic developments that facilitate their call and assist them in good faith to move forward with confidence.

Synchronicity as Affirmation

Immediately following the mystical call, it is customary that an act of synchronicity, which serves to validate the call, occurs. Just as the camp counselor told me that God had instructed her to speak to me about my call, others also report uncanny experiences immediately following their experience.

This is illustrated in Pavarti's experience: "While praying at the altar in my home parish, I felt an utterly strange sensation come over me. I had never felt anything like it. I suddenly 'knew' God was present. I could feel something from outside of me move toward me. Absorbed into this Presence, [something] like a powerful wave washed over me. Then, a voice spoke and instructed me to become a nun. I was left shaking, disoriented, and in a different realm in time and space that I did not understand. I must have momentarily lost consciousness. I could not believe this was happening, although the experience was more real than anything that I have ever known. I stayed at the altar and tried to pull myself together as I got my bearings. I then asked that God give me a sign. I knew that what I had experienced was utterly real, but I wanted to make sure that I understood the practical assignment. I wanted to be confident that the vision and voices to be a nun were not manufactured in a moment of madness or religious reverie."

Pavarti then rose from her knees at the altar tremblingly, headed toward the church exit. "Before I reached the sanctuary door, I heard a telephone ring. I spotted a telephone in the very back of the sanctuary, and alone in the quiet church, while still disoriented, I answered the ringing phone, something that I had never done while visiting the church. The call was from a Mother Superior of a convent in another city in India. She was calling to invite me to enter the convent."

For Karl, following his encounter with the angel at his farmhouse in upstate New York, he was invited by a friend to join her for a Catholic mass, a service he had never previously attended except for a couple of weddings many years before. Despite Karl's fourteen-year hiatus from the Protestant church of his youth, he agreed. Following the service, his friend introduced him to a visiting theology professor who, in the course of the ensuing conversation, recommended a book to him: "Shortly after meeting the theology professor, I found myself in a set of circumstances that were completely inexplicable: I turned down a street I rarely walked and staring back from a bookstore window was the very book recommended to me, which cost the exact amount of cash that I had in my pocket. Cardinal Newman's book, *The Development of Christian Doctrine*, was the confirmation of what was going on. Every line was a blow of clarity and truth. This was a communication to me, exactly what I needed to hear at exactly the right time and provided the guidance I needed to receive and follow the call. How would I have happened to walk down the street in which this very book was in the window display and cost the exact amount of money—to the penny—that I had in my pocket?"

Sometimes the remarkable synchronicities seem fantastical, magical, and miraculous, but such is the power that is described with each call. Not only does synchronicity offer reassurance immediately following the actual call, the frequency of synchronistic events increases as one seeks guidance and assistance to fulfill it.

Here I am reminded of Surjia's story. As a child in South India, Surjia asked for a sign from God, a kind of proof that the call she experienced at the tender age of ten was true. She wanted an event to verify that these other realms of reality she was experiencing were beyond anything that she could create in her own mind. While she did not doubt the mystical experience that called her to serve children, she feared that the guiding voices following the call were all in her imagination and she longed for reassurance.

Surjia reported that invisible forces showed themselves in a direct and miraculous way to commission and validate her experience. Surjia had adopted an abandoned newborn pigeon when its mother was shot and killed by her playmates while playing with a slingshot. She named the baby pigeon Daryl. It was during this time that Surjia prayed for a sign to substantiate the continued messages that were guiding her in her mystical call. In prayer, she heard a voice ask, "How about if I take Daryl from you?" To this, she responded, "You can't do that, if you are only in my head; my thoughts alone."

The following morning her father, a physician, invited her to go with him to pick up medicine in a nearby town. Remembering the voice, she placed Daryl in a tightly woven peacock cage with food and water with a large padlock attached to the door. After carefully securing the padlock, she placed the key around her neck. Yet, when she returned, Daryl was gone. The cage was empty. Surjia's family all witnessed this occurrence and everyone was speechless and stunned. From this point on, she moved in steadfast faith that she was working with forces beyond her comprehension, defying the laws of science that she understood.

These acts of confirmation and synchronicity are common, not only immediately following the mystical experience, but have been shown to continue throughout the life path in pursuit of the call. Beyond the synchronistic events that facilitate the call, there is a growing recognition that the call has its own energy system and meaning. Essentially, the call is autonomous and has its own electrical patterns; it is believed by Jungian analyst Marie-Louise Von Franz that the physical world is activated by the power building up in the psyche, and the mental and physical energy systems co-create synchronistic events, a notion commonly examined in the world of quantum physics. Consequently, each call is shrouded in its own energy system and ignites acts of synchronicity identified in the larger physical world. Such events suggest that the individual is a mere human vessel who carries the power, intent, action, and consciousness of the call into the world—and as this coalesces, the physical world responds.

The Changer and the Changed

CHAPTER 9

Between the conscious and the unconscious, the mind has put up a swing: creatures, even the supernovas, sway between these two trees, and it never winds down. Angels, animals, humans, insects by the millions, also the wheeling sun and moon; ages go by, and it goes on. Everything is swinging: heaven, earth, water, fire, and the secret one slowly growing a body. Kabir saw that for fifteen seconds, and it made him a servant for life.

—Kabir, *translation by Robert Bly*

Not only do remarkable, cryptic events continue in support of one's call, but also the experience and assignment changes the personality of the individual in the process. As one embraces the responsibility, a range of personal changes begins to occur. While the changes are unique to each individual, there are shared archetypal themes that ribbon their way through the lives of those who have said "yes."

The Call as Conversion

The New Testament story of Saul speaks directly to the dramatic and sudden conversion experience. On the road to Damascus, Saul was met with a blinding light and heard a voice call out to him (Acts 9:1–31). Note the aftereffects of Saul's experiences, which carry the same elements of the contemporary stories: Saul saw a light and heard a voice, identified the voice as a spiritual being (Jesus), changed his name to Paul, left his work as a tax collector and preached love as a way of life. Friends and acquaintances believed that Saul had gone crazy. But in time, Paul, like shamans and medicine people from days of antiquity, went on to prove the truth of his experience and demonstrate the wisdom that he had acquired. Paul continued to receive revelatory visions and teachings that shaped early Christianity throughout his lifetime.

At a glance, it would seem that Paul had a near death experience, like P.M.H. Atwater's concept of near death-like experience, when certain types of altered states similar to near death events occur, but actual physical death is not a threat. This seems to be the case with Paul who had an instantaneous change in consciousness and underwent a religious conversion.

As a result of the mystical call, sudden and miraculous conversions are common. Those who already believe in God are more confident and seek deeper understanding, even as their current views are challenged to incorporate the power of the mystical event. Devout atheists have a sudden change of heart and acknowledge a sacred reality. Agnostics claim a new certainty. Literal interpretations are examined anew and the meaning of symbol and ritual takes on new life. Everyone grows more interested in understanding and embracing other faith traditions. Such sudden spiritual and religious changes are frequently disruptive, a steep climb in the journey of individuation.

Following Karl's encounter with an angel in his farmhouse in upstate New York, he reports, "In the spring of 1992, I went from being a very anguished and troubled non-believer to becoming a Christian overnight." This statement reflects the immediacy of the changes resulting from his call to believe in God and become a Roman Catholic. While his conversion in belief was sudden, his relationship with God and Roman Catholicism was an unfolding process that led him to become a different person, step by step. Prior to his revelation, Karl described himself as "...a very immature, self-indulgent, defensive, and unhappy person" who was binge drinking and settled into a marriage characterized by "accommodation and the problems associated with it." From the immediate "turning" to Christianity, Karl's life began to change.

Today, his commitment to the Roman Catholic Church and sobriety are the cornerstones of his new life. He and his second wife received annulments from their prior marriages and their union is now recognized in the Catholic Church. And while Karl's wife is not a practicing Catholic, he feels supported by her in his response to being called.

"The miraculous, the unexplainable has entered my life and continues to do so. There's no greater or more transforming experience," Karl claims. He speaks of the process of "opening" and how that process began on the very day he was called. The opening requires shedding "another layer of resistance that can be very painful, but there's a sense of growing, depth, richness, and scope ... to understand more and more who I am ... a period of struggle, beauty, and clarity followed [being called] with a freedom that's just inexplicable. I am infinitely less fearful, apprehensive, and defensive. My relationships with everyone in my life have changed as a result of hearing the 'call,' particularly those closest to me: My wife, my son, my parents, my siblings, in-laws, friends and colleagues."

For Karl, finding faith allowed him to be less anxious and

socially awkward and fearful. As a result, he is more vulnerable—and, therefore, more intimate and real. This has brought him deeper friendships and growth in family relationships. Furthermore, as if he has grown new eyes, his capacity to see the beauty in nature as well as in his students and passersby on the streets is an entirely new experience for him. He describes a life infused with experiences of synchronicity and daily epiphanies that guide his life. For the first time since early childhood, Karl no longer feels alone and abandoned in a detached and random universe.

Monday morning classes no longer find Karl dulled from a weekend of heavy drinking and tracking the class time on his cell phone, eagerly anticipating the end of the day. Now, he arrives with lightness to his step after attending morning mass, has eye contact with students, knows their names and is engaged with his teaching material, not only as a fascinating intellectual activity that he always valued, but also as the fabric of a growing relationship with each student. Karl is learning what it is like to feel deeply for others, including others who have nothing to give him. It is as if he woke up to the meaning inherent in each interaction. He reports these stories with a deep sigh, as if his anxiety is now leaving and he can relax around others for the first time.

Karl's story reminds me of Tom's conversion to Roman Catholicism, which also happened overnight. Tom was twenty-seven years old when he experienced a multi-sensory mystical call to the priesthood in Gainesville, Florida. For Tom, he would need to leave his Methodist roots, separate from his fiancé of two years, and relocate to a new area of the country. Initially, he was intoxicated with the outpouring of love that he experienced following the call and began reading everything he could get his hands on about Roman Catholicism. He quickly discovered that the Roman Catholic tradition provided the fundamental religious doctrine and rituals that nurtured him after his call. What Tom described as an "unconscious, intuitive understanding of a larger pattern to the universe became rooted in a religious history and a way to conceptualize a more personal relationship with a merciful Godhead."

At the same time, Tom struggled and suffered deeply to end his engagement. He sought support from the local priest, all the while fearing that he would appear foolish, even crazy, given that he had never attended mass prior to being called to the priesthood. Still, Tom never doubted that God had spoken to him on a star-studded night in Gainesville and he was determined to follow the mandates of his soul.

Some roads to greater consciousness traveled down traditional routes, while others led the unsuspecting pilgrim to unfamiliar ground. One such story is Maggie's, when at age thirty-four she left the Roman Catholic Church and her New York City home, following her directive to Japan to study Zen Buddhism. After six months in Japan, she again received a visitation from an angel and was directed to India. There, she studied in an ashram for another six months. For Maggie, a direct knowing of God revealed itself through studies in Asia after leaving the Catholic Church and beginning a committed meditation practice in far-off settings. Through her studies, she soon embraced a universal religious perspective and now revels in discovering all world faiths.

As a shy and fearful child who tried to follow the rules of the teaching nuns at her parochial school, Maggie recalls her visceral anxiety hearing of hell and purgatory. She now understands that her physical self knew that she did not believe all that she heard. Through Zen Buddhism and Hindu philosophy, she feels a spiritual freedom that opened her heart to peace, which quieted her mind and healed her body.

Today, Maggie heeds her call by teaching meditation to physicians and other health care professionals in major hospitals around the country, fulfilling her call to "serve the heart through the freedom of a quiet mind."

Another conversion story is that of Anjali, a thirty-seven-year-old East Indian woman who grew up in the Nazarene–Methodist Church, a fifth-generation Christian. Following her mystical call, she immediately adopted a universal view: "one God and many paths." Leaving the conservative traditional belief system of the Nazarene Church allowed her to follow the guidance she heard. She was told to leave her current religious views behind and know the salvation of true freedom that transcends one particular religious path. Anjali receives spirit guides who direct her path. The first guide presented itself as Buddhist, followed by other guides from Sufism, Judaism, Christianity, and Hinduism.

Following her guides, she met and married her husband, a Hindu. Together they attend the Unity Church, a Christian metaphysical church that embraces all paths. Today, Anjali's understanding of God is "a visceral energy that I can feel as it enters my body, leaving me intoxicated with love and guidance for each step."

Medieval mystic and theologian Meister Eckhart taught that "God does not work in all hearts alike, but according to the preparation and sensitivity he finds in each." This is particularly apparent in the diverse beliefs and lifestyles that are captured in studying the mystical experience.

Kylie, a practicing Sufi, says that even before being called, she had thrown out "that old patriarch in the sky," but since her mystical call, she has been guided to embrace the masculine and feminine aspects of a divine reality. This sacred energy is both "soft and tender in its beauty, as well as terrifying and explosive." Sufi dancing gives Kylie a direct experience of feeling enraptured that sitting meditation didn't offer. While dancing, she is lost in reverie, in praise of a universal source that blesses and directs her life. Moving in repetitive movements carries her into a trance state where she communicates with other realms and receives guidance. Instructed to "Dance, move, and ask, and it will be revealed" has guided her to address critical life questions as she dances, clears her mind, and invokes surrender and humility. Through images, words, and sudden insight, she receives a visceral sense of the answer. When she follows the guidance revealed to her, she is fulfilled and finds meaning and deeper love. When she is not able to access the answer in movement or act on the guidance given, she looks for her own fear and resistance. This fear serves as the next portal for self-growth as she waits for guidance.

After their mystical experience, everyone professed a search for God, although most denied that they were conscious of seeking a spiritual experience at the time of the call, including the few who identified as being "very religious." Others claim that in hindsight, they were seeking a new way of life, but imagined that it would take the form of a new job, move or marriage.

About half of the individuals interviewed had no religious affiliation at the time of the call. Many of them attended church as children, but left as teenagers or young adults and never returned. Many were agnostics, some were atheists, and others had converted to a different faith from their early life. Few adults were active church members or engaged in religious practices of their childhood. What nearly all individuals had in common was a strong spiritual sensibility in early childhood, even if their families of origin were not religiously oriented.

Linda was one of the few exceptions who reported an active search for God at the time she received the call. Linda was drawn to religious matters throughout her early life, but did not feel free to pursue her Jewish roots given her father's efforts to deny his religious identity. However, in graduate school, Linda was deeply moved by a conversation with a new friend, and found she had a fiery longing for a direct spiritual encounter.

While visiting with another graduate student in her apartment one evening, Linda was shocked to learn that her new friend was actively thinking about suicide. Alarmed, Linda spoke with her friend about God as a sacred reality that she had always felt, even as she had denied her religious sensibilities in early life to avoid conflict with her father. Despite what Linda said, her friend could not be comforted—and at one point, her friend grew increasingly hysterical as she alternated between laughter and tears. Too scared to leave her, Linda stayed the night and tried to console her. Finally, they both fell asleep with plans to find help the following morning.

About two hours later, Linda woke and saw her friend glowing beside her, looking peaceful and radiant. Linda recalls that she was beaming. In a glowing light, Linda wondered, *who am I lying next to?*

"It was like being next to a god. I was trembling with an energy emanating from her. I knew that something huge was happening, but I didn't have a frame of reference for it…. The following morning, my friend looked like a totally different person. She continued to radiate with a loving compassion and pure energy that I had never witnessed."

When Linda asked what was going on, her friend reported an experience of liquid gold pouring into her heart; she thought she was dying. Instead of dying, she experienced a miracle in which God moved into her heart and she knew real peace and pure love for the first time.

Later, while driving home, Linda felt envious, wondering why this didn't happen to her. How could this girl find God? Linda ached with desire to know God and feel happiness and peace. She wanted the joy that she had witnessed on her friend's face and felt emanating from her body. Shortly after Linda felt this whole-body desire, she heard a voice. At first, she was frightened, but as the voice continued talking, she felt the same hyper-alert response as when she awakened next to her friend that morning. Unable to focus in traffic, Linda pulled her car to the side of the road and breathed deeply as she listened to what sounded like a Native American chant. A singular voice became many voices and the words of the chant became clear: "God is real in me. God is real. God is real in me and in my soul. God keeps me whole."

She melded into the sound, losing consciousness for what seemed like a few moments.

As Linda returned to full awareness, she was trembling to the steady drone of the chant. Given the sudden impact, she jokes that the experience was like that of the old Hawaiian Punch television commercial in which the guy is walking down the street and all of a sudden he gets hit in the head with a coconut. In that moment, Linda claims, she glimpsed the vastness of consciousness. For her, it was the beginning. She felt unbound by time and space, enveloped by energy of pure love and a loud pulsing heart that beat with the steady ongoing chant. From that experience, Linda developed an understanding of God unbound by time and space. As the droning continued, she was told to test everything she knows through the reality of love.

Linda believes that she heard the "Music of the Spheres," first conceived by Pythagoras to describe the musical harmony created by the turning of the planets, affected by their relative proportion and distance. The idea has been embraced by Western philosophers for centuries. The chanting mystical call not only gave Linda a specific assignment to serve as a healer to those in need, but served as a healing tonic in her own life. The music inspired confidence and a steadfast presence that she is not forsaken and alone in the world. She feels compelled to follow any assignment that arrives through the music of the spheres, and she has committed her life to the music's instructions.

The morning after her call, Linda dropped out of graduate school, left her job, and broke off an engagement. Alone, without a map, financial resources or personal contacts, she heeded the voice, left New Jersey and headed for Florida. As Linda explains, "the music got me in the car."

It was during this time that Linda also began to see a purple light, which she believes protects her. This, and the continued singing, allowed Linda to move to a new area and trust that she was on a path to healing herself and being of service in the world. Linda recalls arriving in Florida and entering the open doors of a Baptist Church to give thanks for the protection and guidance that she received on the trip south. There, she surrendered her life at the altar, knowing that she was now initiated into a deeper sense of God. She was instructed to awaken to a spiritual path guided by music.

Like others who were guided by synchronicity, so was Linda. She described this period as if she were riding a magic wave. A determining event occurred shortly after arriving in Florida when Linda was introduced to a man who ran a retreat center. A successful scientist working for the Pentagon's Atomic Energy Commission encouraged Linda to attend his classes and helped her integrate the mystical experiences that had brought her to Florida. These classes were enormously valuable to in anchoring the powerful mystical experiences that were calling her. In another synchronistic meeting, Linda met a scientist who better explained the Music of the Spheres, and she also studied the writings of Flower Newhouse, who believes the Music of the Spheres comes to distressed individuals and groups throughout history, "like a pulse that's uplifting humanity struggling to be free." These perspectives gave Linda the confidence to continue listening throughout the years. To this day, the music has never stopped.

Regardless of the religious or spiritual path assumed after the mystical call, everyone held a firm conviction of the reality of God in its many forms and called by many names. Of the stories gathered, I tracked those who left their Jewish roots and became devout

Buddhists and Christians. Some Hindus incorporated Christ as a deity, and in time, some Hindus identified themselves as Christians. Some Muslims became Jewish or Christian. Some Christians became Muslim. Everyone claims a belief in the unseen world and expresses confidence in the essence of each tradition reaching for the wisdom in which all religions are embraced, even as one particular path may offer the direct guidance needed in the unique unfolding life of the individual.

God Language Revisited

Over the years, I have contacted many of those originally interviewed, and without exception everyone stayed true to his or her conversion of belief in a higher sacred reality, even as many struggled to find the fitting language to describe the essence of their faith. A new God paradigm is required to fit each person's firsthand experience. Outdated perceptions of God as the old man in the sky or a kind Santa Claus handing out favors for good behavior were released.

More fitting descriptions of a an expanded image of God were found. Names like The Holy, Mystery God beyond God, The Sacred, The Sacred Heart, Energy, Source, The Numinous, The Eternal, Emptiness, and The Universe were the most common ones used to refer to the Nameless One. Others simply laugh at themselves as they struggle to find a word for the ineffable and rely on silence, nature, and meditation. One storyteller, Ravi, sums it up when he laughs at his own "audacity to believe that a single word could ever describe the energy I experienced when I was called. All I can do is accept the direct experience and surrender to the 'Yes.'"

Scholar Andrew Harvey describes the transformational experience as " ...any authentic mystical opening that brings us to a sense of wonder, a freedom from time's fury and anxiety, and a growing revelation of a far larger and more marvelous universe and a far vaster identity than anything we could begin to intuit with our ordinary senses and consciousness. When we are touched by mystic grace and allow ourselves to enter its field without fear, we see that we are all parts of a whole, elements of a universal harmony, unique, essential and sacred notes in a Divine music that everyone and everything is playing together with us in God and for God."

Harvey, like all mystics through the ages, encourages us to have a daily practice to grow in the glimpse that has been revealed and live the truth shown to us. It is a willingness to live the *yes*. According to Franciscan priest Richard Rohr, the "False Self is no longer a threat or an enduring attraction once you have experienced the True Self ... Once the veil is pulled back from illusion, it is just a matter of time before the system crumbles and we rebuild with the True Self's values and guidance."

In essence, those who experienced a mystical call transcended an understanding of the sacred beyond the countless ways that a personal God perspective offered comfort and meaning through the slings of fortune and the hope of an afterlife, to a view of a mystery and wonder that that pressed for personal and communal transformation. Sometimes, this process did not console but crumble previously held convictions so that a larger liberation of Self could erupt and be jettisoned to fulfill the call administered.

Mystical Assignments from the Unseen World

CHAPTER 10

He who fulfills his own dharma, incurs no sin.
—Bhagavad Gita

True personality is always a vocation and puts its trust in it as in God, despite its being, as the ordinary man would say, only a personal feeling. But vocation acts like a law of God from which there is no escape. —Carl Jung

From antiquity to the present, mystical calls can be identified as specific assignments from the unseen realm. While the mystical experience is by nature an intense and dramatic one, the nature of the call includes instructions that set the course for one's lifework and individuation.

Practical Assignments

The practical assignments take many forms. Some calls are general, such as "dedicate your life to healing others," while other assignments are very specific: "go into this church, speak with the priest and say that you want to convert to Catholicism." Sometimes the instruction is to a specific career or professional task; other calls redirect one's lifestyle, beliefs, or values. Regardless of the nature of the call, the conversion experience is in full tilt and the personality undergoes steadfast revision in response. As the call is heeded, the necessary steps to fulfill the call are the transformative building blocks of the new personality. This process continues to shape one's destiny throughout the life span and even into death as one opens to deeper revelation and understands the meaning of the assignment from a wider perspective.

One example of an assignment is that of Marian, a sixty-nine-year-old Caucasian female living in Illinois. Married with three adult children, she is a visual artist and writer. While Marian has had many paranormal experiences throughout her life, it was a vision during her early years that convinced her that she was called to be an artist to serve and educate others for the purpose of social justice. Using design, drawing, painting and writing, Marian has done just that. Her creative work has been displayed in halls, galleries, and national government buildings, which has inspired countless others and raised large amounts of money for underprivileged youth spanning several decades. Her creative fires continue to burn brightly and reveal deeper and deeper mystical dimensions that guided her work all the way to the White House.

Surjia's assignment was a call to service abandoned children. She came to the United States as a young adult and is now married with two children and works for an international adoption program in Kansas. Growing up in a Christian family in rural India, Surjia experienced many transpersonal experiences and maintained a strong belief in spiritual matters. As a child, Surjia knew the anguish of growing up feeling unloved by her mother. Consequently, when she was called to care for those individuals abandoned and alone, she readily accepted the call. In addition to serving orphans, Surjia was instructed to pray for several hours a day for those alone and in need. Her contemplative life has offered support to thousands, and her work has saved hundreds of Indian children from languishing in poverty.

Bryan is a twenty-six-year-old single African American male who works in the field of hospital administration in New York City. He has held a strong sense of a spiritual reality since childhood, although his family life was not a religious one. His mystical call instructed him to leave his current post in New York and become a priest in the Roman Catholic Church. He accepted the call and quickly made arrangements to begin seminary and fulfill his assignment.

Joanie is a fifty-one-year-old Caucasian female who works as a social worker and spiritual teacher in California. She lives alone, has never married and has no children. She grew up in a middle-class Catholic family in Detroit, Michigan. Catholic mass was a regular family event and she was educated in parochial schools. Despite the longstanding Catholic indoctrination, Joanie responded quickly when she was called to study Hinduism and give her life to the study of Shaivism. Adopting a range of devotional practices that have guided her life led Joanie to teach yoga and live an ascetic lifestyle. After receiving the call, Joanie made the study of Shaivism her life's focus. Shaivism is a branch of the ancient form of the Hindu god Shiva in Cambodia and Kashmir, India, and it has required extensive travel and study for Joanie to be educated and fulfill the call. When she is not in Asia studying, she lives simply and dedicates her life to the homeless while teaching yoga at community centers and in prisons in rural Nebraska.

(As acts of synchronicity showed themselves immediately after she experienced the mystical call to live a celibate life and give herself to the study of Shaivism and yoga, she surprisingly inherited a large sum of money from a distant cousin who had no heirs, which allows her to dedicate her life to her call without financial worries. Joanie continues to live in the same small apartment in a small country town in northern Nebraska since she was first called twenty years ago.)

Doris is a sixty-two-year-old British woman who lived a successful "first" life as a litigation attorney, wife, and mother. She made significant career contributions in the United Kingdom, and enjoyed social and sporting activities. Following her husband's automobile accident and subsequent death, Doris had a series of transpersonal experiences, including a vision, hearing voices, and life-changing dreams in which she was called to give herself to the journey of spiritual awakening through self-knowledge. The mystical call was so powerful that Doris retired, relocated to a nearby city so that she could participate in regular psychoanalysis and Judaic studies, as instructed by Jesus in a vision. She has acquired a new name, converted to Judaism and lives a quiet contemplative life, making regular pilgrimages to Israel.

Durga is a forty-seven-year-old Indian woman who lives in New Delhi where she grew up in a well-educated urban family. She attended college and pursued a career in writing and publishing until she received a mystical call instructing her to change careers. Following the call to be a leader in political and judicial reform, she took the necessary steps in the complex justice system and was the first woman to become a police officer. In time, Durga has held increasingly powerful law enforcement positions, which afforded her the opportunity to make significant reforms in the country of India.

These brief profiles offer a glimpse of the varied lives of those who have been called. However, no synopsis of the actual practical assignments captures the multi-faceted experience of what is required when surrendering to the call. In part, this is the nature of the complexity of any singular life. Essentially, each individual is challenged to honor the Latin adage *Omnia mea mecum porto*, meaning "all that is mine I carry with me."

The Autonomous Power of the Call

The experience of the call is believed to be powered by an archetype, an invisible energetic force that houses it own autonomous energy center and system. In this regard, the individual does not carry the weight of the call alone. In essence, when the assignment is heeded, one begins to recognize that the call has a life and spirit of its own, which shapes the individual as much as the individual gives life and shape to manifesting the assignment. The mystical call becomes the changer and the changed.

Perhaps my own story illustrates the archetypal energy that is carried in the call, beyond one's own personal agency. As a child, I interpreted my call as an assignment to be a Christian missionary, a voice to teach and work in India. This literal understanding was the only framework that I knew as a child in the evangelical and, later, Baptist traditions.

As my own theology was reworked in adulthood, I had a keen sense that my call to service would be fulfilled in my work as a psychotherapist and psychoanalyst, which for me is its own form of community ministry. Here, I could help others understand their unique destinies and sacred centers. And still, even as this work has been steadily fulfilling, my early call to serve in India never left my peripheral vision. Only in hindsight can I identify the archetypal energy patterns that were presenting themselves in a parallel process to normal waking awareness.

Somewhere between grace and effort, I glanced the movement of God's tender hand when I submitted my application to adopt a child. Despite that I made no special requests pertaining to country, race, or heritage when I decided to adopt, I was assigned to a child in India. Suddenly, I felt the rumblings of my early call, intuitively knowing that my work in India was still waiting.

Upon arrival in India with my five-year-old daughter Hadley

and two supportive friends, we had plans to complete the adoption and then travel for a couple of weeks before returning to the United States. Our trip was abruptly changed when we arrived at the hotel. Here, armed police officers and media personnel greeted me with accusations of child trafficking. I was staggered by their unwarranted questions and rattled by the fact that they knew personal information about wide-eyed Hadley, who was looking on. Soon, I learned that the authorities had seized my adoptive daughter's documents when a successful sting operation arrested the two kingpin leaders of an underground human trafficking ring in Asia. Furthermore, the police had closed the orphanage that housed my daughter, Annaporva, then eight months old, and transported the babies and children to an unidentified government holding facility. Annaporva's adoption papers were signed by the same social worker who had been caught purchasing female infants for the underground ring, and the arrested leaders' names were on her documents. The entire orphanage staff was arrested and jailed and Annaporva's whereabouts were withheld and adoptions in the area immediately banned.

In time, I was investigated and forced to defend myself in an unfamiliar legal system in what became a highly publicized national case. Strong public sentiment about international adoption, the caste system, the devaluation of girls (as indicated by the three orphaned males per one hundred girls), and attitudes about Western adoption compounded the outcry against human trafficking, to which I was publically accused. By the following day, my face was plastered on the front page of Indian newspapers. The faces of the heads of the closed orphanages joined mine in a hysterical feeding frenzy, with the press, politicians, and police eager to blame someone. While the men were held in jail, I was the public figure to be harassed, as it was believed that I was involved as a transporter of purchased children from India to the West. Angry strangers threatened my life, and when I sought counsel from the American Embassy, I was directed to leave the country and abandon my plans to adopt my child.

While the American Embassy offered no practical assistance, one staff member offered a sage warning. He informed me that while slipping out of the country would be the prudent thing to do, I would leave knowing that it would be nearly impossible that I would ever again locate and adopt this particular child. With no computerized record keeping, or documentation of the babies shipped to various holding facilities, the passing of time would make it increasingly impossible to locate and process the necessary documents that would result in an adoption. Even if I stayed, with an immediate ban on international adoption blanketing the area and the children moved to undisclosed locations, there was no way to be confident that I could find Annaporva, prove my innocence, and leave the country with her—but now would be the only chance for that. The American Embassy staff members encouraged me to weigh all of these factors, along with the physical threats, personal stress, and financial costs and make a decision that I could live with. It was sound advice.

When the situation looked quite dismal, a fortuitous meeting led to the kindness of a Catholic sister who advised me that the only person who could offer clearance and political protection to search through the government orphanages was Maneka Gandhi, Indira Gandhi's widowed daughter-in-law. The younger Mrs. Gandhi served as the Minister of Social Justice and Empowerment, based in New Delhi. We all slipped onto a night flight from Hyderabad to Delhi with plans for my friends and Hadley to leave the country while I pursued a meeting with Ghandi. This was the beginning of a string of synchronistic events that stretched out before me.

Locating the Office of Ministry of Social Justice and Empowerment, I joined the long line of individuals waiting in the oppressive India sun for the periodic opening of Gandhi's office door to admit as many individuals as could push their way across the threshold before the guard resisted the crush and again pulled the door closed to loud groans of disappointment. During one such opening, the guard shouted out to me above the rushing crowd flooding through the door. In perfect English, he called out, "When I open the door again, stretch your hand out as far as you can high above the crowd and I will try to pull you in."

Hours later, exhausted from the heat and the deafening raucous of the New Delhi streets, I spotted the door beginning to swing open. I pushed through the overheated bodies and grew close enough to reach his long extended arm and was yanked through the blanket of bodies through the open door. I will never know why the guard at Gandhi's office door reached out to me, but his hand made all the difference.

Arriving breathless into Mrs. Gandhi's dark outdated office, I heard first a disharmonious choir of sobs and shouts ringing through the broken windows that lined her wall. In front of her oversized desk, which was barely visible under mounds of paper, the group of us that made our way in was motioned to the rows of chairs lined before her and instructed to speak our respective concerns when addressed.

When Gandhi motioned that it was my turn to speak, she was fierce in her response. She announced unequivocally that she did not want to be associated with this international intrigue but would arrange for a staff member to meet me at the New Delhi airport at 6:00 p.m. that very evening with a baby and all the necessary adoption documents and travel papers to depart immediately on a U.S.-bound flight.

I pulled out a faded photograph of Annaporva. I told Minister Gandhi, "I don't want any child, I want my daughter." I tried to hand her the photo, but in disbelief that I had refused her offer, she yelled in outrage, added flailing dismissive gestures, and continued down the row of individuals pleading their respective cases.

Stunned, I listened speechlessly to more desperate pleas presented. Some of their stories stayed with me. One elderly frail gentleman sat stooped in his chair as he requested funds to build a nursing home for the elderly in his village: "The young people have gone to the West to be educated and never returned to care for us." A veterinarian from Goa made an eloquent request to purchase additional donkeys; he also needed medicine to treat animals with back injuries from the weight of hauling supplies up the mountain roads.

I pieced together their stories spoken in English with Hindi and other languages and dialects woven in. I feared that soon we would be ushered out, and my chances to get my daughter were dimming as the requests were ticked off on Gandhi's note pad. Then, with no indication that she'd had a change of heart, Gandhi picked up her heavy, black rotary-dial phone and placed a call. With the same strident temper shown toward me only moments before, she began shrieking at someone on the other end of the call: "I don't care what it takes, I want you to keep this American safe and help her find this baby."

Dazed, I was then ushered out of her office, instructed to return to Hyderabad where I would be met at the airport and escorted in search of my daughter.

Her last prescriptive words drew the line: "The rest is up to you."

The following day, I traveled with the police, swarmed by the press, and located Annaporva in an abandoned, dilapidated building that formerly housed government offices. Followed by photographers and journalists, I filed past women washing the orphans' clothes in street puddles and placing them to dry on nearby bushes. I quickly realized that this decrepit building had no running water, kitchen or washing facilities and was housing one hundred infants in filthy conditions. It is no surprise that thirty-three of the hundred children died within the first month of being transferred to this makeshift facility, a casualty of adult grift and corruption.

I walked slowly through the rows of worn but colorful low-lying cribs, trusting that I would recognize Annaporva from the videotape provided by the US adoption agency months before. Near the dirty broken window, a baby on her stomach lifted herself as her large chocolate eyes met mine. I knew this was my daughter. The number on a tag tied to her crib matched, but I didn't need the confirmation: I knew this was Annaporva. With Maneka Gandhi's permission, I was allowed to transport my Anna in the convoy of police and press officers to the clean orphanage on the outskirts of the city overseen by the Catholic sister who had originally guided me to Gandhi. After my daughter was settled, the police waved the press onward, and they disbanded, leaving me alone with Sister Teresa.

After locating a vacant crib, Sister Teresa guided me across the grounds to a row of nearby buildings and into an adjoining hospital. Following her up several flights of back stairs, she then entered a near-empty hospital floor and led me into a room darkened by black paint-colored windows and a big padlock on the door, all carefully arranged for me. Here, I was assured that I would be protected from the onslaught of the press and threatening calls.

It had become clear that the ordeal was far from over. Hadley was now safely back in the United States and in the care of my parents and I began to slip in and out of the country, traveling between my two children. Annaporva was eight months when I found her but she didn't leave India for ten more months. First I had to endure a court battle to prove that she was relinquished voluntarily and that I was innocent of any wrongdoing in the trafficking of children.

The bounty of synchronicities was in full motion, but even

then, I was unaware of how my mystical call was weaving through these dark days. It seemed that nothing could be done but stay out of the public view and hope for good news from the string of lawyers; some merely pretended to be of assistance, only to disappear from view after demanding hefty bribes, while others fought tirelessly.

During these long days of waiting in a hot hospital room, I returned to my research on mystical calls, even interviewing the nurses who had been granted keys to deliver daily rice, and water to my room. One trusted nurse served as a lookout when I exited the hospital through stairways and back passages, which led to the orphanage so that I would visit with my Annaporva in the evenings. Sometimes, I would go to the orphanage and, hiding her in a blanket, bring her back to my room and reappear with my happy bundle in the early-morning daylight, avoiding a public sighting. Other days, I was able to keep her with me throughout the following day when I didn't need to slip out for legal meetings.

Annaporva was with me on one particular auspicious morning. The nurse who oversaw my care inadvertently left the padlock hanging on the outside of the door, leaving the door unlocked. Without knocking, two men burst into my room carrying a large brown bag and began querying me as to my name and the child I was holding. Given the newspaper articles and uproar in the streets, I feared that they were there to kidnap or kill me. Shielding Annaporva on one arm behind me, I met them with my own questions, trying to stall for time in hopes that the attending nurse may return and assist me. When questioning them, the more talkative man announced that he had heard a "call from God" and was guided to find me. My fear reached a fever pitch when the leader reached deep into the brown bag he was carrying. I was suddenly frozen, imagining that he had a weapon of some kind. The two men stood blocking the door. Steadying my body as a shield for Annaporva behind me, I began trembling, uncertain what may lie ahead.

My fear deflated as suddenly as it had risen when the intruder pulled out an enlarged and framed picture of Annaporva and me that had been in the local papers. Holding the picture across his chest, he introduced himself as a Christian pastor and announced that he had been called by God to begin a ministry named after me. My understanding as to why the pastor pursued me is related to the discrimination that many Christians experience in India. The pastor claimed that "only the love of God would lead a rich white American woman from a Christian country to adopt a low caste abandoned orphan." Convinced that he had received a call from God, he now wanted to receive my blessing. Weak with relief as I tried to wrap my mind around his words and comprehend that he was not going to harm us, I collapsed on the bed and told him that I would need to speak with him when I could think clearly. With arrangements to be in touch, he departed and I was left with my mind spinning at what had just transpired. It took a few days before I could gather myself and grasp from everything that he had said in those few moments that he, too, had a mystical call. His "affirming synchronicity" was that he found me. To this day, I still don't know how. In continued correspondence from the United States, I grew increasingly convinced as to the authenticity of this pastor's experience.

I provided no funds, but it seemed apt that the outside publicity over Annaporva's adoption be converted into a force for good. I sent a letter with my blessing to begin a church named The Green Ministries, as requested, but suggested that the seminary be named after my father, given that their religious beliefs were more consistent with my father's, and the school be named after Annaporva.

A year later when I preached before a large gathering under a thatched roof in rural India, a "Green Ministries" banner waved in the spring wind. I felt the power of my childhood call and a sense of its fulfillment. Although I grew to interpret my call to service beyond the literal confines of a missionary, the Green Ministry now includes several churches, an outreach service project, and a school, all having nothing to do with my direct effort.

To me, this illustrates the impersonal and invisible assistance that fosters the manifestation of the call, often in spite of one's own conscious intent. As if the mystical call has its own archetypal power, aided by unseen forces, a larger Mystery is witnessed. Some believe that ancestral Spirits or angels guide such uncanny events. Some believe that it is part of a preordained path. I was merely bearing witness to the numinous and following the guiding star of destiny.

Whatever invisible forces may be operating when one heeds the call, remarkable events take place—of this we can be sure. Doors once closed begin to open; resources appear in the face of scarcity; needed connections spontaneously occur.

As I documented hundreds of mystical calls that found their way to my door, my own faith in the meaning-making nature of the world grew stronger. While one person leaves a successful career to enter rabbinical school in mid-life, another inherits a million dollars to support a life of study and volunteerism; yet another receives public acclaim for art effortlessly selected for display in the White House.

Extraordinary stories of mystical calls continued to find me, even as my own call was still unfolding.

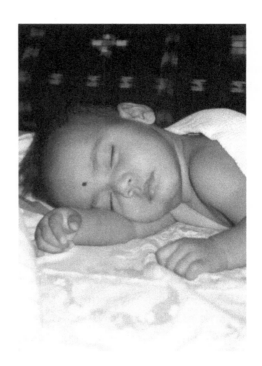

Transformation

CHAPTER 11

The Golden Age Is in My Heart Today

Who are you, any one, who can remain unmoved
when the Light breaks upon you?
Who can say it is just as well not to see as to see?
Who can ever be the same child or woman or man
again after the Day has broken?
Who can admit that there is anything else in the
world, after this has come to the world?
And though I was very sorrowful having to leave so
many friends behind, I did not turn back;
For when the soul is once started on the soul's jour-
ney, it can never turn back ...
Can you now go on with your old life as if nothing
has happened;
The whole universe has happened;

—Author unknown

Seek not for love but rather seek to remove from
within yourself the blocks to the awareness of
love's presence, which is your natural inheritance.

—Rumi

A New Frame of Reference

For those who have been called, a different philosophical perspective begins to unfold. It is a deeper listening to the soul that overrides the time-bound everyday desires. Following the call, the hungry ego is held in its valued and necessary place in relationship to a larger Self. From this perspective, interests and life goals typically change. Some interests and attitudes effortlessly fall away. Other changes require discipline and time.

During this time, the necessary courage and stamina required to carry the weight and responsibility of the call begin to form. Depending on the individual's personality style, different demands will present themselves and require different emotional and spiritual muscles unique to each assignment. For example, when Elena was called to leave her corporate marketing position and work with AIDS patients, it was necessary for her to go beyond her self-serving lifestyle. Elena admits that the responsibility of the call "scares me to death," as her life no longer is about *her, her* family, *her* friends and *her* belongings, but about the population that she was called to serve.

The gravity point, once anchored in ego identity, is now shifted to the *Higher Allegiance* as referenced by Oxford scholar Evelyn Underhill. The demands and desires of daily life are still present, but they do not hold the same weight and focus as before. They are not central. This new reference, for lack of a more fitting term, is by nature, religious—not in a dogmatic or restrictive sense, but through continued revelation that grows out of a relationship to something beyond oneself. This becomes the spiritual life, "costing not less than everything," as prophesized by poet T.S. Eliot.

Bertrand Russell, English mathematician and philosopher, claims, "The gate of the cavern is despair, and its floor is paved with the gravestones of abandoned hopes. There Self must die...for only so can the soul be freed from the empire of Fate." Thus, "costing not less than everything" is the hard work that the conscious seeker faces and a journey that is rarely embarked upon.

This hard path, described by philosopher Alan Watts from the Zen perspective reminds us that Zen is not always a gentle breeze, "...more often than not, it is a fierce gale that sweeps everything ruthlessly before it, an icy blast which penetrates to the heart of everything and passes right through to the other side!"

Despite the transcendent indicators that nudge one on to a new orientation of Being, the demands and pressure placed on the personality to die before one dies to find a new way of being is the hardest work one may ever encounter.

The arduous nature of the path is not only one of surrender and finding a true contextual understanding of what has occurred, it is a learning curve in which one begins to incorporate what has happened in the various domains of one's life: the psychological, behavioral, spiritual, cultural, and global meaning. Every transcendent experience must be integrated on all aspects of one's understanding, lest one is left with a mere self-serving psychic experience that falls flat. This is the hard work of true transformation.

A Moment in Time

The actual moment in time, the date of a call frequently becomes an anniversary in one's life span, not unlike a wedding anniversary or the birth of a child. Sultan Valad, the son of Sufi poet Rumi, claimed, "A human being must be born twice, once from his mother and again from his own body and his own existence. The body is like an egg and the essence of man must become a bird in that egg through the warmth of love, and then he must go beyond his body and fly in the eternal world of the soul."

The timing of the call occurs serves as a point of demarcation in one's personal narrative: a spine in the book of one's own life that holds the pages together. It can also serve as a frame of reference. The far-reaching personal changes that result from the call leave some individuals feeling as if they have lived two distinct and separate lives, one before the mystical experience and one afterwards. Time as one previously experienced it has collapsed under the weight of divine intervention and a new beginning.

This new life is not without sacrifice and grief, for leaving the past is always a complex move, no matter how inspired one may feel going forward. The necessary loss of what will remain unlived must be faced in the transition, even as one hopes for the meaningful life that is summoned. For some, grief weaves through the changes as the unlived life is sacrificed and mourned. Like the Sufis that teach us "to die before you die," many who experience a mystical call admit that they had to euthanize their current life to give themselves over to the waiting path. Both Jesus and the Buddha point to the renouncing of the false self, a dying process of the ego as the spiritual path unfolds. This is the foundation of the new frame of reference that occurs during this transformational stage and marks this moment in time, unlike any other.

For example, when Tom was called to be a priest while sitting on the hood of his car outside of Gainesville, Florida, he left behind his earlier life with his fiancé, work in the medical field, and active membership in the Methodist church. The call quickly became the defining moment in his life—and he grieved for his former life, even as he proclaims, "I was given my life" that night.

Zander, a young married attorney practicing in Boston, emigrated from Singapore with his family when his father was transferred to a position in Chicago. Educated in the United States, he and his wife reported that they were happily married until Zander experienced a mystical call during a weekend getaway to Vermont to enjoy the fall foliage. Climbing to a nearby vista point to over-look the brilliantly colored landscape, Zander suddenly felt nau-seous and dizzy. He steadied himself against a towering maple and then slid down the trunk, resting on the bed of leaves below him. Zander's memory of the event is partial, but he recalls staring at a golden maple leaf and felt his body merge with the maple leaf as it quivered in the warm fall breeze. Experiencing himself as the golden leaf fluttering on the stem of this giant tree, Zander was blinded by the brilliant sun shining through the dark branches. He remembers trying unsuccessfully to sit up, again giving in to the colorful ground below him. Mesmerized, he didn't know if he was the leaf, looking at him; or was he, himself, staring into the life of a leaf? And then he heard the words, "serve the Sami people." At that point, he felt flooded with a well-being he had never known, and floated in the warm afternoon sunlight as if the sun itself was pure love and goodness.

Although Zander had never heard of the Sami people and was initially too disoriented to research the subject, he began to have dreams of reindeer and curiously, overheard a group of people dis-cussing the Sami people in a delicatessen when he returned to work the following week. Researching the Sami people, Zander learned about the Laplander tribe in northern Scandinavia.

Over the coming months, Zander scoured everything he could get his hands on about the Sami people and their history in the north country of Norway, Sweden, Finland, and the Kola Peninsula of Russia. He learned about their culture, language, art, reindeer husbandry, as well as their economic, social, and political status in Scandinavia. Two years later, Zander left his legal firm, endured a painful divorce, and enrolled in a course on the Sami people at the The Centre for Sami Studies at The Arctic University of Norway.

Today, Zander commutes between a home in Stockholm and the Swedish university town of Uppsala, where he serves as an advocate for land rights and reindeer husbandry alongside international advocacy rights groups affiliated with the United Nations. The revelation under a maple tree on a Vermont fall day changed his life in ways that he never could have expected. His grief was tremendous as he walked away from his previous life (and the prospect of children) and began his life anew—a life that Zander now describes as a "deeply fulfilled, albeit a very different and sometimes lonely life."

Zander dreamily comments, "I forget my former wedding anniversary, and some years my birthday slips up on me, but never the day when I was shown a new way of being. It is a responsibility as well as a gift that I had to grow into, both psychologically and spiritually. I must surrender and listen every day. I am part of a living miracle. I was born again on the day The Divine spoke to me. And to think that, prior to that day of Mystery, I was an avowed atheist."

Zander's statements speak to the message that religious scholar Paul Tillich taught when he held that the resurrection is not limited to an event some future day but is the power of the New Being to create life out of death here and now..."

Time's Paradox

In addition to a new frame of reference and the changes in priorities and attitudes, there is also a change in how one experiences time after the mystical call. The assignment is always weighing on the individual—whispering, shouting, pulling, and tugging at one's heart. Often, there is a sense of urgency to take action. As a result, time in general is commonly experienced differently. Some describe a mixture of excitement held within a more spacious relationship with daily life. One described the new experience as living between the urgency of passion, while feeling quieter at the same time. Time itself is measured differently and one's relationship with Kronos is altered, living in the space between the tick and the tock.

Having crossed a threshold in space that some know as "liminal," a Latin term from the word *limen* that refers to crossing into a sacred realm, forever alters one's perspective of time.

The call invited Zander to relax, trust, and surrender into a spiritual domain after leaving his post as an attorney in Boston. His high-powered "type A" personality style required that he learn to meditate and still his racing thoughts. As he grew in his meditation practice and steadily moved toward fulfilling his assignment, a new relationship with time emerged. "Managing the weight of the vision has shown me that I have to 'hasten slowly,' as the late Laurens van der Post prescribed: pause, reflect, and listen to life in a way that I had not known before the call. I experience my life within the context of time very differently now."

Practically, this evolving relationship with time changes one's choices and priorities. Time spent in longstanding personal interests and hobbies may be redirected to matters that pertain to the call. Some interests previously enjoyed are no longer valued. Living a balanced life of love, work, play, and creativity are pillars that Jung holds for whole living, but what may have been perceived as balanced before the call is now different. Play must not be lost, however; it is the unique nature of play that often keeps an individual close to the foundations of the unconscious mind, where the energy pool of the call resides and must be nourished.

Relationships in Transition

Not only do religious, philosophical, and spiritual views change following the call (as well as time, interests, and priorities), but relationships, understandably, are deeply affected.

Megan described her life changes as sudden and abrupt after

she was called. She had previously lived a busy and fulfilled life of travel, professional lectures, and intellectual activities in a university town with many good friends. After the experience, Megan relocated to New York, entered Jungian analysis and committed herself to her spiritual journey, as directed in the vision she received. In reflection, Megan says, "My husband and I used to travel with other people, sightseeing or golfing. Now, my time is consumed with activities that support my call. I travel with a group called Goddesses and visit the Black Madonna sites and sacred landscapes. My interest in bridge and cocktail parties suddenly changed. I feel a constant urgency to fulfill what I have discovered is mine to do. Essentially, I want to fulfill my call and spend time with those who want to know themselves before they die. It's not that I don't value my treasured friends from the past, but I'm just not interested in the same things anymore. Life changes dramatically after you are called."

Surjia, called to serve the orphaned children of India, acknowledges how hard it is to juggle her work and time between the needs of her own children with the soul-crying pressure to find placements for millions of waiting Indian orphans. Surjia receives steady guidance and strength from dreams and spirit guides and discusses her call openly with her husband and children. She asks for their understanding and is grateful that her marriage has survived given the priority of her call.

The Longing for a Sacred Love

For many, there is a newfound longing for a Sacred Reality. The mystical experience created a hunger for what was unrecognized previously but is now known and embraced. The words of St. Francis depict this immeasurable desire after a mystical encounter:

Dear God, please reveal to me your sublime beauty
That is everywhere, everywhere, everywhere.
So that I will never again feel frightened,
My divine love, my love,
Please let me touch your face.

The longing for the Divine is commonly experienced when one has surrendered to the call and falls in love with a larger vision. It is a time in which the erotic breath of an infinite mystery has set a flame burning—and once felt, there's a longing to know more. This flame is fueled by a living relationship, often experienced as being in the presence of an ancient witness. This relationship reveals the peculiar bond between the small self and the Ultimate Purpose.

The Timing of the Call as a Determining Life Factor

How one wears the cloak of the call is not only shaped by one's personality style, psychological capacity, social, cultural, and life circumstances, but the physical age in which one receives the call influences how one adapts to the experience. It is a different learning curve and life trajectory if one receives the call in childhood or early life. Fewer lifestyle changes may be required if one receives a call when single, without a spouse or children. However, with family responsibilities and all the accoutrements of midlife, often including a mortgage and work responsibilities, relationships are often more complicated to manage after hearing an assignment.

Those who are called as children, as in my situation, have their own unique benefits and challenges. The obvious benefit is that a child's identity is more malleable and unformed. On the other hand, an early call may shape a child's identity in challenging, developmental ways. A child may immerse him or herself in a religious or spiritual orientation with a devotion to God that separates her or him from contemporary youth culture, leaving a child feeling different and alone. Interests in school, extracurricular activities, hobbies, friends, and dating relationships are largely determined by how these activities fit into one's call. As a result, the child who is called may develop differently and follow a different trajectory in life than other children. It is not surprising that my best friend at age six was twenty-six, and that as a teenager I had a refuge at an elderly blind woman's home whose door was always open to me. Older friends understood my concerns in a way that peers could not.

Young mystics may date, but typically hold back from making commitments and getting married, appearing quite ambivalent in love relationships, as their primary love relationship is to their call; their lover is God. In fact, mate selection may grow increasingly complicated. Attraction and personal compatibility are valued qualities of a prospective partner, but these characteristics are secondary to how a prospective mate fits into the called life. This holy longing creates foremost questions in the young mystic's mind. Does Spirit or God's will lead this choice? Is this the Sacred Marriage that will enhance my call?

As a young adult, I recall going on double dates with peers, only to return home and feel baffled as to how others could find such pleasure in activities that left me bored and empty. For young people who are living a mystical call, mate selection based on simple attraction and shared activities, without soul-searching for the shared larger destiny, holds little interest.

Therefore, those who experience a call as a young person may not follow the conventional path that is typical of adult development: dating, marriage, career, household and parenting tasks, and retirement. Rather, those driven by the star of their call from an early age tend to address such developmental milestones later in life. This can lead to an identity crisis in mid-life or later when they realize their common life stages are unlike their peers. They must reckon with that which was lost or sacrificed along the way. Few models exist for people touched by their daemon - that supernatural energy that moves between mortal and divine reality, early in life. The longing for the Eternal overrides date night.

It is no wonder that many who are single at the time of being called remain so. They know the sentiments of the poet Rilke, "I want to be with those who know secret things or else alone." In my own situation, I was deeply conflicted about committing myself to anyone given my private devotion to the Divine and all that it entailed. Some single individuals feel confident that a supportive life partner can be found, but worry whether daily contemplative habits will fit into marriage or family responsibilities. Many individuals express their need for solitude since meditation and prayer can be time consuming. Some individuals wish they were called to a religious order or community, so that they could enjoy the support and friendship of shared values rather than juggling secular life and the demands of their call.

For those already married at the time of the call, a different set of challenges arises. Lifestyle and career changes influence one's partner and children as well. Some spouses feel abandoned or resent the new life their partner now claims. Some spouses describe a loss of control, given it wasn't a life choice that they had anything to do with. Some spouses privately admit that if they had known such a life-changing mystical event would have occurred, they might have made other choices in mate selection. Other couples grow apart, living parallel lives in daily activities and interests, even as respectful understanding exists. Some marriages end as one's spiritual life takes on deeper meaning and with increased time demands away from the family.

While some spouses fail to understand or relate to the mystical call and the aftermath of personal changes, others identify with the changes and are supportive. These spouses feel the weight of the mystical call on their marriage, but witness its power in the life of their spouse and join in the larger journey, recognizing that a private daemon is at work. They recognize their supportive roles as significant, and value the personal growth that occurs on this exceptional life path.

New Gifts and Abilities

Another documented change that follows is the frequency and intensity of transpersonal experiences. From prophetic dreams to visions and ESP experiences, daily life is often colored by extraordinary moments. Learning to manage them becomes part of the challenge of working with energies that present themselves in other forms. The mystical path impacts friends and family members.

For some, a particular type of psychic ability becomes more dominant than others. This was the case with Joan, a young accountant who was called to work as a foster care mother to nine children. Shortly after being called, she developed an enigmatic connection with those dying. This happened for the first time with a work colleague. Joan was waiting in her car for her mother to join her so they could go to a local concert, when suddenly she heard her friend Leon's voice saying, "I want to tell you that everything is all right. Do not be afraid." When Joan returned home from the concert later that evening, she received a call informing her that Leon had been trapped and died in a fire in Washington, D.C. earlier that evening. She remembers it well: "The hairs stood up on the back of my neck, for I recall looking at my clock on the dash of my car when Leon came to me. It was the very time of the fire."

Other stories reflect an enhanced capacity for the paranormal in general, as reported by a friend, Katie, who described the mystical call as something that "completely disrupted my life even as it inspired it, and afterwards, I became tremendously psychic. I would meet someone and know all about her or him, before they disclosed any personal information. It was like having a halogen light bulb in my head. I could see light all around and in people. Sometimes this was frightening, but I learned to work with it and not take myself too seriously. I believe my brain changed from whatever happened during the call, and developing psychic abilities grew out of the experience."

As the years passed, Katie has learned to manage these intense experiences and reflects, "When you first experience it, it's a huge leap, like a bridge you have to cross, but now, it just happens and feels like a natural occurrence. I have spontaneous visions. I don't even think twice about them. They aren't as disruptive. Usually they make sense. If I don't understand them, I'll write them down and simply track them. Sooner or later something will happen that shows me their meaning. It may be revealed through someone I meet or something I read, or in a dream or vision. These experiences become a continuous fabric. They have a saying in Zen that 'the two worlds are separated by the width of a hair.' Living at this depth in daily life requires that I stay open to each moment, forget about my persona and how I fit in. The call, and all that has happened since, offers me the support to be more of who I really am."

World religions scholar Huston Smith reminds us, "It is traits, not states, which will serve us." Transpersonal experiences demonstrate different states of consciousness, but it is the developing personal traits that are of value. One must attend to such experiences with a light touch and avoid identifying with the abilities as a quality of value from the perspective of the ego. The ego can take most anything and misuse it. Such a misstep only serves inflation and the deeper transformative work is weakened. Without sufficient consciousness and perspective to hold the increased abilities that develop, there is a risk that spiritual gifts become cheap commodities and bolster one's identity and pride. As written in the Bible, "Ye will know them by their fruits." Traits, not states, matter on the spiritual path.

As stated before, integration of transcendent experiences are crucial if one is going to live a whole and holy conscious life. Otherwise, particularly as it comes to psychic phenomenon, such experiences can easily be applauded, feed the ego, and no real development occurs.

Finding Meaning in Suffering

Alongside the shift in religious perspective, sense of time, personal relationships and an increase in transpersonal experiences, this changing life orientation fosters a search for meaning in both everyday experiences and life's ultimate issues. Finding meaning in both pleasure and pain, and health and suffering, supports an increasing self-inquiry and objectivity about life's journey. Suffering, while not invited, becomes another milestone to be lived in life's great paradox: beauty and horror; peace and anguish; fighting for and letting go. Accepting one's personal suffering supports a willingness to take one's place and find meaning in the larger universal story of human suffering, especially as it contributes to fulfilling one's call.

If one sufficiently integrates one's call and continues to climb the ladder of consciousness, there is increased insight that evolution is directional, which offers a new map of human suffering. A worldview of chance is weakened and evolution as a directional process is recognized. Michael Meade speaks of evolution as a meandering process that includes dissolution and rebuilding in its process toward increased consciousness—and that impacts one's map of meaning-making on the personal and collective domains.

Surjia found such meaning in her childhood suffering. Raised by a mother who was heartbroken to have a daughter, Surjia was sent off to a boarding school while her brothers remained at home with the family. "I am a motherless child, even though I have a physical mother." Surjia claims that while her mother treasured her brothers and other children, particularly underprivileged children, she never connected with her. She describes her mother as a devout churchgoer and valued member of the larger community who would come home and "beat the crap out of me." While this has been a source of tremendous emotional pain for Surjia, she believes that it prepared her for "everything I have done. I think it is because I didn't have a mother to run home to, I found a kind of freedom and ventured out to where I wouldn't have otherwise traveled. Rejected, abandoned and abused in early in life has fueled my understanding of the meaning of my call and made me who I am so that I have great compassion toward other children in need." Now, Surjia feels called to pray for those "who have no one else to pray for them, especially those children mistreated and abandoned.

According to twentieth-century Afrikaner author Laurens van der Post, who was also a farmer, an advisor to British heads of government, and godfather to Prince William, "Meaning transfigures all: and once what you are living and what you are doing has meaning for you, it is irrelevant whether you are happy or unhappy. You are content. You're not alone in your spirit. You belong."

Freedom from Fear of Dying and Belief in the Eternal Soul

Just as one's interpretation of suffering is altered as one climbs the rocky terrain of consciousness, so is one's attitude toward the end of physical life. Once melded with the Divine, if only for a split second, one rarely fears the physical death of the body again. Stories of freedom from fear of dying were bountiful from the old and young in all traditions. I will forever remember the peace that I felt while speaking to my vision of Jesus and musing how anyone could be scared of death after being touched by Mystery.

Raymond Moody's seminal work in near-death experiences (NDE) identifies nineteen key elements, most of which are reported after mystical calls. P.M.H. Atwater has identified four different types of NDE, three of which also share similar characteristics with mystical calls, including access to otherworldly dimensions and scenes beyond the individual's frame of reference where revelations of great truths are communicated. The most common qualities that mystical calls share with certain types of near-death experiences are the out-of-body experience, the encounter with light, an encounter with someone, and a greater acceptance and peace in the face of physical death.

Along with a change in relationship to personal and global suffering, one's relationship to end-of-life issues, including death, is transformed. In my visit to heaven as a teenager, all fear of dying left. I returned convinced in the reality of an afterlife. While each person interviewed had different understandings about what happens after death, everyone believed in the reality of the soul and its journey to be reunited with a larger Source following the death of the physical body. While the deep grief of missing someone in physical form may remain; the fear of life's finality is released.

Naturally, the "eternal soul" and the continuity of life will be shaped by the particular practices and traditions that best sustain each person's interpretation. For some, the soul is the psyche, housed in the depths of the unconscious life, released into Spirit when its life purpose is complete. For those who follow the teachings of Tantric master Nisargodatta, the soul merges into beingness as it moves into spirit and it bursts with utter bliss. Nisargodatta taught that God is an *indwelling* principle, awakened at the moment of death. Just as the cow's udders ooze milk upon seeing its calf that runs to her summons, so does the Universal Spirit shower grace when awakening to its pure essence at the time of death.

From the Sufi tradition, at the time of death all properties return to their original substance: fire-to-fire, water-to-water, and earth-to-earth. The soul awakens in this process and merges with the Infinite.

In the Jewish mystical tradition, the soul is understood as the eternal aspect that was once unified but became fragmented and broken, splintered into millions of pieces across creation. The time on earth allows the soul to gather itself through its search for the soul's meaning. The lost soul fragments are found both inside and outside the individual. Meaning is found in a lifetime of gathering one's true spiritual identity, which invites the soul to become whole again. The period on earth is then complete and it is time to face God, where a relationship with the Sacred Energy of Being continues.

For Christians, having immersed oneself in life on the earth, redemption is the act that reunites the human soul to the eternal. Christians envision the soul living on in a heavenly domain with God forever.

Those who identified as Hindus, Buddhists, and Muslims also adopted a view of the continuity of life, either in reincarnation to work out the soul's lessons or in a larger cosmic divine state.

In death, as in life, there is a deepening understanding that Spirit is in action in physical form and beyond. It is understood as creative force that is built into the very fabric of the cosmos.

Community and Service

Regardless of the specific assignment, there is a growing recognition of the importance of the larger community and how one identifies with the "family of things," as poet Mary Oliver describes. Similar to the philosophical shift from one's personal interests to the purpose-driven life of meaning and allegiance to a higher calling, there is movement from a self-referential framework to one that encompasses the larger community. As this happens, the desire to be of service expresses itself.

An increased awareness of the larger human family grows into focus, although one's actual assignment may be a solitary activity. Some assignments require active collaboration; others are solo, introverted practices. Regardless of the physical activity, the value and intent embrace a wider view of how humanity is serviced. In fact, it is possible to say that the healing power is weakened when one loses this vision and isolates oneself as if his or her purpose is for oneself, alone. The mature psyche knows this—the one who is called, lives it. Being of service opens a whole new door to life's abundance, which heals the wounds of the ego and fosters the next rung of spiritual growth.

In general, a shift outward supports a more fulfilled life, which serves a dual purpose: one lives a more whole life, but also fulfills the terms of *dharma*, a concept in Hindu philosophy that points to the unique law of one's being. One's call—no matter how solo or public the tasks may be, how introverted or extroverted in personality style—is performed with an eye on the local and global community.

From a Buddhist perspective, the role of community, or the Sangha, is a central cornerstone of one's practice. Buddha is held as the enlightened teacher of the Dharma, or truth realized, and the life of the community is that which keeps one strong along the way.

The notion of community is not limited to one's immediate circle, but also the historic and global connection of one's life. Essentially, the development of individual consciousness cannot be separated from the larger cultural, social, and political currents of one's life. Calls link every generation with visions that shape culture and the collective consciousness from antiquity to the present. Priest Martin Bell conceives of it as if "...the courage of Karen Silkwood adjoins the intentionality of Cesar Chavez and links up with the vision of Albert Einstein, which reaches out to the commitment of Martin Luther King, Jr." The ancestors are calling, linking consciousness and action across time.

Love as a State of Consciousness

As one is transformed by the mystical call, one is consistently challenged to stretch into the most determining characteristic that drives us: a consciousness of love. In fact, this is at the heart of the aftereffects of the call. Love is not the feeling-state typically defined before the call, but a state of consciousness that arises toward the whole of humanity, after the call. It is an attitude of being; an orientation toward the world, including oneself. This fundamental change in how one loves and experiences love creates an enhanced sense of personal liberation, which has its own power and peace.

This growing consciousness of love may be influenced, but not determined, by one's religious, spiritual, cultural, or personal orientation alone. Unlike sentimental feeling, the state of love is experienced as a state of *being*, an energy field of consciousness. It comes with discernment and right action, not driven by emotion, pride, fear, and guilt. The energy field of love, rooted in compassion, gives way to joy—even states of ecstasy and peace that deepen as one grows spiritually.

The central energetic archetypal influence of love is experienced either during or immediately following the actual call. While some people experience awe and terror during the mystical experience, they quickly find themselves bathed in an energy that they can only describe as love. Familiar descriptions include: feeling awash in love, held in love, encountering the face of love, drowning in a sea of love, and relaxing into the arms of love.

I recall the words of my friend Joy-Lynne about her experience of being called as a young child: "There appeared this magnificent image, so brilliant I could hardly look at it … Here was this wonderful loving image reaching for me and I had this feeling that I was very loved and I was being called for something. I felt a total sense of awe, love and at peace, knowing that God was calling me into a life of service to give to the world. I never doubted the reality of love again."

Helen, an eighty-four-year-old Texan who had visions of Jesus, spoke of being "bathed in the most amazing love. It lasts as long as three, or three and a half, days and gradually loses its hold. To hear this, it may sound like a manic episode, but rather, it is a deep peace even as I could explode from the energy of love I am experiencing. One wonders if this mystery of love and freedom have always been present, but it took a mystical experience to receive it, as if the voice I heard were a plea to remember myself."

Marc, a twenty-nine-year-old man living in Scotland, describes the moment of being called as one in which he "could explode trying to hold this [love] in my body." Although Jewish by birth, he reports that Christ came to him and asked if he had any questions.

"How can I have any questions? I'm amazed you're here."

The Christ figure responded, "In regard to your world, if there is anything you can lose, it's not real. Test everything against love.

Nothing is worth a grain of sand compared to that feeling of our eternal nature."

Tom remembers his call having ecstatic qualities but "first and foremost, love. Now I understand that God is love."

These reports are consistent with the work of contemporary mystical scholar Andrew Harvey. Harvey describes total communion with the cosmos is experienced as an overwhelming sensation of love, even as other intense emotions circle round.

This experience of love is identified in all mystical traditions. Be it Kuan Yin in Taoism or Jesus in Christianity, there is the centrality of love; building a new construct that transcends "an eye for an eye" to "turn the other cheek." Through the Christ Spirit, the mercy of the Mother Mary and the Holy Spirit, the experience of love and the creation of a consciousness of love and compassion are central.

In the Hindu tradition, the elements of love and compassion show themselves as nourishment and sustenance personified through Vishnu. Vishnu feeds and sustains the mystical soul and gives birth to Lakshmi, who like Jesus, is seen as the beautiful companion and helper on the path. We see the mystical love in Buddhism as the Bodhisattva Tara, along with many other forms that exist purely to help liberate every living creature and free them from suffering.

In Judaism, there is Shekinah, an in-dwelling feminine mother who guides us through life's turmoil and helps us find our way back home, until we rest again in Mystery. Regardless of the religious tradition, it is the power of love that calls out to us—and in the intensity of the mystical call, this voice challenges us to return to our source.

Social Action

As one's focus and value of the larger community grows in tandem with compassion and living in a state of love, attention to matters of justice is a natural outgrowth. Franciscan priest Jack Jezreel recognizes how wide the spirit of love spreads when he writes, "We are either a people who love, embrace, and enter into a caring posture with our family, friends, neighbors, strangers, and even enemies (real or imagined) or we will spend our lives mercilessly trying to define who is lovable and who is not, who is worthy and who is not, who deserves my attention and who does not. Inevitably, we will end up loving people who look like us, think like us, and pledge allegiance to the same flag—and we will exclude the rest. In this truly useless pursuit, we will separate ourselves from God (through tribal worship), from the world's good (by avoiding healing and restoration), and from our very souls (through self-preoccupation with ego)." This, in a nutshell, instructs us in the ways of love when we surrender to a Higher Allegiance.

The mystical call bridges psychological development, spiritual insight, and social action, regardless of the particular assignment. Any separation of psychological health from spirituality, and spirituality from social action is understood as a false claim. It is the interweaving of these aspects that fulfill the call and the individuation process, as Jung indicates. These processes are, in fact, one and the same.

The call is increasingly understood as a conversion of *being*, wrapped in a call to action that goes beyond one's own ego-driven goals and needs. This requires sustaining right relationship with the sacred dimension through whatever spiritual practices that nurture the soul. While the mystical call typically occurs privately, the living of it always expands to the larger world and is refined through right action. To that end, the call challenges healthy living in everyday relationships. Methodist founder John Wesley holds that "There is no holiness without a social holiness."

To that end, the growing path of the call is not only a realignment with placing oneself in the larger community and learning to love, it is a justice-seeking, speaking-truth-to-power compassion. These qualities fuel behavior that is the mystic's social action. This has its own weight and responsibility, requiring discernment of daily yes'es and no's; self and others; inner replenishment and outer action. This is the constant reckoning in living the call from the depths of what has been revealed to oneself while living in relationship to one's family, neighborhood, community, and world. In essence, mystical experiences support action that is transformative, a healing of the whole.

Even a glimpse of the cosmos in its pure energy radically transforms an individual into a more compassionate person in response to the suffering of the world. It beckons a re-orientation to life as it is known. The heart begins to hold more joy as well as pain. There is a deeper connection to all humanity while also increasing sense of difference as a result of being called. One grows every more present to the paradox of the road one is traveling: a heightened feeling of one's bond to the cosmos and therefore, a tremendous sense of belonging—and simultaneously, a sharper contrast in being different separated from mainstream contemporary culture.

Feelings of connection and loneliness co-exist for many who have been called. Daily life becomes easier and harder. On one hand, the comfort of the invisible world is as close as one's breath, while the labor to fulfill one's assignment is arduous.

If we avoid the engagement of community and the collective suffering, the ego may trick us to believe that we are fulfilling the call, but the soul will be left hungry. Refusing the call like the

Biblical Jonah will leave us hiding in the belly of the whale, a symbol of living in the shadow.

In summary, an encounter with the Mystery makes it possible to transcend those materialistic, approval, and status-seeking drives to expose the soul's hunger to be known and manifested in living love and right action. As scholar Evelyn Underhill declares, "To know this at first hand—not to guess, believe or accept, but to be certain—is the highest achievement of human consciousness, and the ultimate object of mysticism." To this end, all religious, cultural and psychological blocks that prevent the development of liberation of the soul beckons us to heed what has been heard and the light that has been shown. This beckoning continues to call out from one's soul throughout the life span to the soul's transition from this physical form into Spirit.

PART III

Transcendence
or Madness

CHAPTER 12

*If you repress what you harbor, you will be stifled by
your own unlived life. You must find another way to
come to terms with your opponent while you are on
your way to court.* —Fritz Kunkel

While more work is needed in the fields of consciousness and mental health to understand transpersonal experiences—and, in particular, mystical experiences—significant headway has been made over the past century. We are on the cusp of understanding everyday transcendent experiences as well as further reaches of mystical states given the research that has popped up in many different fields of study. Experimental drugs in this century have bridged with ancient religious practices. Humanistic and transpersonal psychology has found its bearings in the Western teachings of Jungian psychology. Jung's exploration of the unconscious supports greater acceptance of Eastern philosophy. The neuropsychologists have touched the new field of neuro-theology, and physicists have joined hands with religious leaders to forge a clearer understanding of far-reaching states of consciousness. Over the past several decades, they have challenged the medical and mental health status quo to examine transcendence states of wellness, creativity, spirit, and illness.

Religion and Psychiatry

Until recently, the fields of religion and psychiatry have remained in separate corners in the discourse of altered states. In fact, mental health practitioners have received little to no training in addressing different states of consciousness or spiritual and religious concerns. Likewise, the clergy have received limited diagnostic training in mental health, restricting more seminary training to a general study of pastoral care.

However, the bridge is now being built, as leaders in these respective disciplines recognize the human need to understand transcendence and mental health from a more unified perspective. In time, the hope is that this awareness will spread out to everyday practices and the layperson's awareness.

In January 1993, Pope John Paul II and the president of the American Psychiatric Association, Joseph English, met and commenced a dialogue about sin, God, healing, and health. According to Shorto's report, they met eye to eye on fundamental points of the nature of the human condition and the role of religion in psychiatry and psychology. Both agreed that a full understanding of the individual must consider the spiritual dimension and the capacity for self-transcendence. Word of their meeting was spread around the world and served as a milestone in transforming a bias against religious experience that has been inherent in the fields of psychiatry and psychology from its inception.

Freud's classic definition of religious experience as "regression to primary narcissism" was challenged, not only by those in the alternative movements of Humanistic Psychology, Transpersonal Psychology and New Age spirituality, but by the figurehead of the old guard. In the line of inquiry of William James, Richard Maurice Bucke, and Carl Jung at the turn of the century, the human person as a religiously sensitive entity was finally acknowledged. Humanistic and Transpersonal Psychology stood on their shoulders—and in doing so, created a fertile context in which psychologist David Lukoff, along with psychiatrists Francis Lu and Robert Turner, were successful in achieving a career-capping milestone: They won the necessary votes within the American Psychiatric Association to add the "religious or spiritual problem" to the Diagnostic and Statistical Manual of Mental Disorders (DSM) fourth edition in 1994. The very fact that this category is identified confirms that religious and spiritual matters exist and deserve to be taken seriously.

This work opens the door for individuals who experience mystical states to be properly treated and avoid mental health problems that result from being misdiagnosed, but rather assisted so that they can integrate the experience. Mystical experiences with images and voices from other realms may drive what began as a mystical event into a deep spiritual crisis, leaving the individual bordering on madness and lowering one's capacity to function in society—with few places to turn for understanding.

Astute philosopher and author Ken Wilber emphasizes that transcendent states of consciousness demonstrated "...by the rare, the elite, the ahead-of-their-time—might actually give us some hints about what collective evolution has in store for all of us tomorrow." Without adequate research, insight, and training to work with such states of consciousness, an entire range of wisdom and inquiry into the human mind may be lost.

I recall seeing a neurologist after a minor head injury from a car accident in my early twenties. After the perfunctory examination, he surprised me with a series of questions that sounded more like those used in a standard mental health screening:

"Do you hear voices? Have you ever seen lights or colors? Have you ever been instructed to do something by a voice from some-one who is not physically present and identifiable? Have you ever known something that rationally, there is no way that you could have known?"

Alarmed, I chose to lie to him rather than risk being labeled—or worse, involuntarily hospitalized. Staying calm, yet eager to leave his consulting room, I heard him call out to me as I reached for the door. Turning to face him, I paused, and he gently said, "Danielle, I know you are lying to me, but it is all right. You are a healthy and strong young woman."

I choked in surprise at this unexpected response and blurted, "How did you know?"

He told me that he'd recently attended a neurology confer-ence in Rome in which psychic phenomenon had been discussed. Reviewing my MRI and EEGs taken after the car accident, he saw that my brain registered high alpha and theta states, which are consistent with deep states of relaxation, meditation or light sleep, while I was alert to my environment. He explained that high alpha and theta brain waves occurring while one is fully alert might indi-cate psychic phenomenon. This wise elder physician gave me a gift by explaining TPEs from a neurological perspective, providing a biological base for my experiences and normalizing my differences. I was one of the fortunate ones.

Rather than mental illness, some research in the fields of quantum mechanics, physics, neuroscience, and the new field of neuro-theology suggests mystical calls and other transpersonal experiences may be forerunners of the next evolutionary step of the changing brain. More sophisticated instruments and research are needed to test hypotheses that some brains may be wired for extrasensory or transcendent experiences. In the same way that some animals differ from other animals in their capacity to hear, see, smell, or sense their environment, some individuals may have keener senses or perceptions than others. Some individuals may be multi-sensorial according to the research of Dean Hamer, and wired for experiences of transcendence more than others. Without sufficient understanding, or awareness of altered states of consciousness, individuals who are living more evolved multi-sensorial lives can be misunderstood. Such misunderstanding and a failure to support their differences can lead to its own form of psychological distress and social isolation. Absence of documentation is not necessarily absence of truth.

Transpersonal experiences dating back to ancient shamanic practices and Greek sleep temples, which are now understood as hypnotic states, along with the work of William James at the turn of the past century, have noted the biological changes that occur as a result of altered states. In *The Varieties of Religious Experience*, William James identifies common characteristics of certain types of religious experiences, including voices, lights, visions, automatic movement, and hallucination. Along with involuntary vocal utterances and difficulty breathing, episodes of loss of consciousness and (on rare occasions) convulsions have been documented. James noted that some of these experiences were accompanied by bodily changes, spontaneous healings, loss of sleep and appetite, a radically new nature, feelings of ecstasy and jubilation, loss of worry about the future, and the ability to see other realities. These reports from the turn of the century as well as those in the past fifty years speak of the power of transcendent states and the psychological and physical effects of the mystical experience.

Neurobiological and Personality Changes

William James' work is increasingly confirmed by contemporary studies in neurophysiology. In deep meditative states, mystical experiences, near-death experiences, and certain types of other transpersonal phenomenon leave a residual effect on the workings of the brain, as well as the personality.

Through the use of the electroencephalogram (EEG), the amount, rate, and rhythm of electricity in the brain can be measured and serve to document the changes that occur in altered states. As one's rate and rhythm of electrical currents are altered, so is brain functioning, as indicated in the use of neurofeedback for attentional difficulties, anxiety, and depression.

In addition to electrical circuitry that may be altered with deep states of consciousness, so is the rhythm of the heart, breathing, and temperature. The heart works more like the brain than previously believed and the intense nature of the mystical call is shown to impact the heart. Not only are there more mood-shaping hormones found in the lining of the guts than the brain (all the more reason to have healthy bowels!), but the heart converts one form of energy to another as it generates messages throughout the physical system. The instinct and intuition pulsating from the body's core may register and send energy before the conscious mind can process the incoming stimulation or threat.

Given that the major glandular system and the electromagnetic field are five thousand times greater than the brain, the heart and the bowels are likely the most determining systems of the quality of life. This discovery, placed in the framework of evolution, clarifies what Charles Darwin recognized when he wrote that love and moral sensitivity are more important in the evolutionary process than the survival of the fittest or natural selection.

Furthermore, deep structures in the pineal gland, limbic system, pre-frontal lobe activity, and DNA are all areas of medical inquiry that examine how different states of consciousness influence one's biological functioning.

There is reason to believe that the plasticity of the brain, along with other documented changes, are cumulative. And of course, like all neuro-biological changes, this shift in one's physiology modifies behavior and attitudes. These changes are not only adapted into brain functioning that alters one's quality of life in the present, but are seen as traits that are passed on to future generations. In this regard, certain altered states of consciousness, deep hypnotic and meditative states, along with mystical ones, leave a residue that contributes to the evolution of humanity. In DNA research led by scientist Emma Whitelaw, physical marks of an experience and their aftereffects are traced in the DNA. Here, we begin to understand what the epigenetic researchers know in claiming that our biography becomes our biology.

On the other hand, increasing documentation points to the genetic and biological bases of spiritual experiences. Distinctive brain processes shape how one experiences transcendent states of consciousness. It appears that higher consciousness is, in part, determined by the structures at the base of the brain. The frontal area of the brain is encoded by the ability to construct sensory data and process cognitive information. These distinct circuits are interconnected but vary among individuals in significant ways. According to scientist Dean Hamer in *The God Gene*, different versions of the gene VMAT2 inform how the monoamine, a transporter mechanism, signals and influences mood and perceptions. One version of this gene offers only a limited feel-good signal to the base of the brain. Another version of this gene creates an enhanced flow of serotonin, dopamine, and adrenaline to the base of the brain and creates a dramatic shift in the communication between the front and back of the brain that fosters an overwhelming mood of joy and peace.

Essentially, a spiritual experience can be triggered by a genetic influence that creates a rush of feel-good hormones to be released when there are certain triggers. For example, one person sits in church and makes out the grocery list, feeling peaceful but emotionally neutral.

Another is swept up by the sacred music and awash with peace. Each person may be coded differently by the versions of the gene that is believed to influence how hormones are moving through the system and creating a strong communicating circuitry between the cortex and parietal lobes. To this end, some brains are more wired than others for spiritual and mystical experiences.

At the same time, it is common knowledge that some types of mental illness display visual or auditory religious hallucinations and compulsions and obsessions. Given that some of these features can be identified with certain types of mental illness, it is appropriate to examine the relationships between mental illness and transcendent states. While true mystical experiences by an individual without indicators of mental illness may be more easily identified and understood, it is not so simple to distinguish mystical states of consciousness when they are threaded through more complex pathology. This only substantiates the need for further research. Nonetheless, even in the face of mental illness, who is to say that bona fide mystical experiences did not take place and hold meaning in the context of that individual life?

Without adequate ego structure and well-functioning neurology, a tipping point may erupt into illness. Or, perhaps some geniuses step into cosmic or invisible realms but, unable to incorporate such experiences into normal reality, slide into madness. As Isaac Newton stated, "I can calculate the motion of the heavenly bodies, but not the madness of people."

As more extensive medical research is conducted, it will be useful to understand how and why some individuals experience a mystical event that fosters a life-enhancing breakthrough, while others tap into madness. Increasing research suggests that some brains that are wired for mystical experiences may, under certain influences, flip into mental illness. In fact, individuals like Isaac Newton, John Nash, and Florence Nightingale are among those noted for their genius, yet they join the ranks of those whose brilliance also displayed mystical responses congruent with illness.

This is not to suggest that a mystical experience predisposes one to mental illness in and off itself, but rather, the importance of assisting one who has transcendent experiences to receive useful assistance as needed so that one knows how to interpret and integrate such a far-out event is a valid research and clinical consideration. At this point, research lacks sufficient data to distinguish all the differences between a bona fide spiritual emergency and a psychotic episode.

In summary, the impact of spiritual and mystical experiences cannot be minimized in the evolution of our species. And yet, without adequate interest and research into transcendent states, fundamental gaps in medical literature and treatment will remain. This leaves an entire population of individuals dismissed, misunderstood, or underutilized.

Fear of Being Misunderstood

It is understandable why a high percentage of individuals who have experienced a mystical call will not discuss it openly for fear of being misunderstood or labeled as mentally ill, even as they themselves trust the validity of the experience. One such person is Kurt, a sensitive Jewish man from the northeast. Kurt had a powerful mystical experience in which he saw a vision of an outlined man surrounded by a bright golden light. The man spoke to him and instructed him to go to Israel and study a rare sleep disorder, the Kleine-Levin Syndrome, as part of his post-doctoral studies. At age twenty-six, Kurt could not come to terms with hearing a disembodied voice and seeing a vision, even as he reported, "it was the most peaceful and loving experience I have ever known."

Unable to accept "such a bizarre experience that made no rational sense to me," he grew increasingly depressed and went into therapy. His psychiatrist diagnosed it as a one-time, idiopathic psychotic episode that he should dismiss. Convinced that he had lapsed into a moment of madness after a stressful academic term, he went on anti-depressants and anti-psychotic medication and took a term off of graduate school. A severe side effect to the anti-psychotic forced him off to go off the drug, but left him believing that he must be vulnerable for mental illness.

Today, thirty years after the mystical call, Kurt practices meditation and has had several transpersonal experiences. He now professes that he never fully disbelieved in the authenticity of the mystical experience, but the nagging doubt that he was losing his mind was more than he could manage at the time. Convinced that he was vulnerable for madness as advised by the medical establishment, he avoided anything to do with medical research and his interest in sleep disorders. Today Kurt has been forced to revisit Kleine-Levin Syndrome, affecting one in one-million adolescents, when his own son was diagnosed with this rare disorder. In hindsight, Kurt wishes that he would have honored what he now believes was a true mystical call, but he had no frame of reference to understand what had happened to him at the time.

Two groups who received social support when they spoke openly about their mystical experiences were members of more conservative Christian religious faiths, which provided literal interpretations of a personal God; or were Asian or of Asian descent, with more accepting, Eastern viewpoints. These orientations provided religious paradigm and interpretation of such experiences that could be integrated into one's personal identity as well as offer the social support and validation needed.

However, even those in conservative Western faith traditions did not feel comfortable sharing all that had happened to them. For example, few individuals shared any psychic developments that emerged from their mystical experience, believing that this would be seen as wrong or sinful in their conservative traditions. They simply told their church friends that they had been called by God to do a particular task and such a claim was not challenged or denied.

Outside of this small group within the conservative wing of the Christian church, many individuals lived their calls shrouded in secrecy. For some, secrecy grew out of their fear of being different since they had never heard of such an experience before it happened to them. For others, there was a fear of receiving undesired feedback or being the victim of the negative projections of others. Consequently, many avoided speaking about the experience and the changes that grew out of the experience. I recall meeting a former Catholic sister while I was attending graduate school and learned that she was uncomfortable being friends with me once she heard of some of my own psychic experiences. For her, these events were believed to be from the devil, and while she did not want to believe this, she was uncomfortable around me.

This was also Carrie's experience. A forty-seven-year-old Greek expatriate living in New Zealand, Carrie told her story for the first time after attending one of my presentations. Her call occurred when she was nineteen years old, and led her to research, write, and publish work on those disenfranchised in modern Greece. She did not worry that others would judge her, but given that she didn't know anyone else who had a mystical call, she didn't want others to contaminate the experience with their lack of information and own interpretations that could be devaluing or misguiding. Now Carrie recognizes that others have had similar experiences and feels more confident in speaking out.

Refusing the Call

There are many reasons why individuals refuse the call. For some individuals, integrating the actual mystical event itself is manageable given their ego-strength and larger view of the cosmos. However, implementing the necessary emotional and lifestyle changes to *fulfill* the assignment is more than they can manage. This conflict alone can mark a life.

One such example is Don's story. At the time of the call, Don was unable to accept the assignment. However, at a different stage of his life, he returned to the call and fulfilled it. I first met Don at age sixty-one, a time when he was facing the call he had received at twenty-seven. Don had the psychological capacity to accept the validity of this vision that appeared to him while hiking in a rugged, mountainous region of North Dakota; it instructed him to help coal miners in Appalachia. Don felt peaceful and in love with life following the call, and therefore, believed and accepted that this was his life's work. However, he had recently married, bought a home in the Northeast, and acquired a good job with an insurance company.

Following the call, Don began studying world religions, joined a Sufi meditation group and attended a local synagogue. He actively sought a framework to understand the vision and the blast of love and peace, which flooded him during and after the experience. Ultimately, Don turned his back on the practical assignment. He said that it was always "on his shoulder" but he was unwilling to turn his life upside down with no guarantees that it would work out. It wasn't until Don went through a major depression in his late fifties after his wife had passed and his three children were grown that he decided to take action and heed the call from thirty years before. Don took an early retirement and, through contacts from his college days, was able to secure a position working with the Appalachian coal miners and their families, the very directive that he had been given on his mountain hike when he was twenty-seven.

Don claims that he now feels a deep sense of peace for the first time in thirty years. He says that he is free of the heartache that he had felt for decades, knowing he wasn't living his true destiny. In hindsight, he sees that he was afraid of what others would think, especially his new bride and her parents. Now, he wishes that he had found the courage to pursue his call earlier in life. Despite the "great joy and fulfillment" he experiences today, he reports episodes of inconsolable remorse that "I wasted time trying to avoid what my life was all about and what I may have accomplished if I had found the courage to accept this path sooner." An unknown seeker once claimed, "Never to have seen the truth is better than to have seen it and not to have acted upon it."

Others believe that they can manage the lifestyle changes and stand up to the disapproval of others, but are intimidated by the enormity of the assignment itself. This was the case with Samuel who worked as a biology teacher in a small town in the south. Called to be a veterinarian and work with diseased cattle, Sam applied and was accepted into vet school, but soon discovered that studies were more demanding than he had originally imagined. This, along with the extra work hours to pay for his schooling and the student loan debt, led him to return to teaching full-time and quit school.

Others abandoned the call after seeking advice from their priests, ministers, or rabbis and found only misguided assistance. This was the case of Sally who turned to her priest after receiving a mystical call as a twenty-four-year-old graduate student. Sally was a French major when a voice instructed her to enter the field of occupational therapy and help those with traumatic brain injuries. Sally found the calling too daunting given that she had just accepted a scholarship to complete her final year of French studies. After three days of feeling disoriented and weak after the experience, she attended mass and asked to speak with her local priest. Although well meaning, the priest did not understand what she was talking about. He assured her that it was all in her imagination and to release such a silly notion and enjoy her French studies. Now that twenty years have passed, Sally believes that it was misguided advice and regrets that she did not heed "the road not taken." Sally illustrates what the poet William Blake framed as "divine discontent."

What becomes of those who do not follow the call, either due to lack of needed guidance and support, or due to getting sidetracked by the demands of daily life and dismissing the call outright? What becomes of those who set out on the path, but stumble and get lost along the way? Regardless of the choices made, the call is a unique journey for each traveler and carries its own opportunities and consequences.

For a few, heeding the call seems effortless, as if the individual's capacity and circumstances coalesce and they slide onto a course of successful action, never looking back. Others embrace the call but stumble and slog through each step as if a weighty endless climb dictates life's movement. Others heed the call unknowingly. They respond to a given situation and discover that they are fulfilling the very assignment that was asked of them.

Given the mystery and uncertainty of the outcome of each call, some wonder if, in fact, all calls should be honored. Are all mystical calls life enhancing or is it possible that some individuals are gripped by a "dark call," which creates harm or destruction? (Perhaps this is one of the more obvious markers in distinguishing mental illness from true mystical phenomenon.) Yet, how does one know if the call is guaranteed to be beneficial to everyone involved? How does one decipher a difficult but life-enhancing path toward the good of one's own development as well as that of the common good, or when one is lost in the shadow of one's own woundedness and disillusionment driven toward an irrational, dangerous, or harmful assignment?

In the Roman Catholic tradition, there is an emphasis on the "discernment of spirits"; deciphering good from evil. Such spiritual rigor is needed when the validity of the mystical call is under review.

There are no easy answers to these complex questions. In part, the answers are not known because the questions have not been asked. While many stories of mystical calls have survived throughout the ages, too few have been systematically studied and tracked through time. One can only surmise that the integrity of the call itself is a determining marker if the call will serve the welfare of the individual and the larger good, even if the experience may be very difficult and a different outcome that one originally envisions.

Provided the call is one that supports the larger integration of the whole, it would seem that even if the call is refused for any of the multitude of reasons, the nature of a loving and redemptive universe has a long arm of justice; the last no gives way to a yes. Or put another way, given the meaning-making nature of the psyche, even the unlived life, which has refused the call, reaches out for meaning and revelation. Perhaps every loss will ultimately open the door for a new encounter that reveals yet another insight on the journey. The descent can also bring new life; a *via negativa* becomes the road that leads to dark wisdom as the mythologist Michael Meade suggests. It may be a path of sorrow but, as the poet Oscar Wilde discovered, "Where there is sorrow, there is holy ground."

Depending on how one perceives and defines the source of the call largely shapes how one frames and interprets refusing the call. If one adopts a nondualistic view of the Divine, then meaning and purpose, even in the call's refusal, is threaded with meaning since the Source or God is The All, Everything. God is found in action and inaction, acceptance and refusal, light and dark.

For Carl Jung, God is showing itself regardless if one follows or refuses the call, as marked by the words of the Spartan proverb that hung over the door of his office as well as scribed on his tombstone: "Called or uncalled, God is there."

Transcendence, Psychedelics, and Consciousness

Some individuals who long to experience transcendent or mystical states turn to psychedelics or other drug-induced states in their search. While this was not the case in this study, it is believed that those who grow to rely on such activities for spiritual guidance and transcendent experiences are usually cheating themselves of a deeper transformational experience. Typically, the mystical experience is not "earned," or brought about; but presents itself as an act of grace.

Perhaps mystical phenomenon is largely determined by one's brain chemistry, as discussed previously, but whatever the source of the mystical experience, it is the aftermath and life changes that distinguish the authentic life of the mystic. Sri Nisargadatta Maharaj held that "Some misguided seekers, with the aid of drugs artificially induce a state of forgetfulness, but this is benumbing the sense by extraneous means. Such people will not have enduring peace, only hangovers and sour heads. If you want eternal peace, you can have it and be it through the absorbing devotional path ...".

For some individuals, a deep spiritual quest is jumpstarted as a result of a powerful drug experience. For some, hallucinogenic drugs opened the door to a sacred view; it was the beginner's step. Unfortunately, most find it is a dead-end and no sustained wisdom is formed unless a foundation is in place to embody and grow from the experience. If the drug-induced state fosters a reorientation toward oneself and the larger life as previously discussed, including psychological insight, a useful interpretation that has been wrestled from the depths, movement towards right action in the world of relationships, and the larger community, there is unfolding wisdom. Otherwise, the mystical experience is reduced to novelty and feeds the hungry ego.

In summary, continued research in the fields of neurology, neuropsychology and neuro-theology will illuminate how transpersonal experiences impact physiology, specifically brain functioning, the endocrine and digestive systems, and the human heart. Such changes, along with the psychological and spiritual ones, provide valuable insight into expanding multisensory abilities that may serve to show us the meaning of mystical calls and contribute to human evolution.

Hopefully, in the study of consciousness, more medical providers, mental health professionals, vocational counselors, pastoral care staff, clergy, spiritual directors and teachers will grow to understand the religious and spiritual nature of the psyche and offer support to those who have experienced a mystical call. Then, armed with greater insight and compassion, we may be more available to those who are fearful, confused, or even lost as they untangle this complex mysterious web. Let us recognize the brilliance and creativity that shows itself in these altered states of consciousness, for evolution according to many theorists is a wildly self-transcending process.

Unrecognized, misunderstood, or mistreated mystical calls that show themselves in the larger community inspire our time and understanding as well. We can only imagine the hospitals and jails that house those who have been unable to incorporate the call, or have been misunderstood or misdirected by well-meaning but unwise helpers, only later to recognize that the invisible world was reaching out to them. Many mystical experiences are treated as psychotic episodes when, in fact, a person may be having a bona fide mystical experience, which cannot be integrated into his or her fragile ego structure.

Finally, the question of transcendence or madness is a vast one—but if studied, may carry us into the next rung of science as the human brain interfaces with the invisible realm of the soul.

A Psychological Interpretation of the Mystical Call

CHAPTER 13

What is it, in the end that induces a man to go his own way and to rise out of unconscious identity with the mass as out of a swathing mist? Not necessity, for necessity comes to many, and they all take refuge in convention. Not moral decision, for nine times out of ten, we decide for convention likewise. What is it, then, that inexorably tips the scales in favor of the extra-ordinary? It is what is commonly called vocation: an irrational factor that destines a man to emancipate himself from the herd and from its well-worn paths. He must obey his own law, as if it were a daemon whispering to him of new and wonderful paths.   —Carl Jung

Facing the power of his own transpersonal experiences, Carl Jung recognized that he had touched the archetypal world—and in so doing, experienced firsthand energetic magnetic pools that influence the psyche. These archetypal vortexes show themselves as universal energy patterns, themes, and motifs that move throughout the collective unconscious and carry a kind of genetic museum, a living storehouse that is held in the grooves of our very being. This invisible energy system, a notion that predates Jung, is now moving into modern psychological thought, and increasingly understood in the fields of quantum mechanics and physics.

Furthermore, Jung believed that some experiences are too complex, both psychologically and biologically, to hold in sustained conscious awareness at this point in human evolution. As a result, some powerful transpersonal experiences flood the conscious mind and leave impressions in the form of symbols and images, unable to be absorbed any other way. Here, Jung placed mystical experiences in an evolutionary context:

"Like little children, we still forget what we were yesterday ... Such a state of affairs is an unmistakable symptom of the youth of human consciousness, which is still unaware of its origins."

The fragile, still evolving physiology when seized by the archetype cannot metabolize and sufficiently grasp the pure experience. It is as if the mere mortal's physical body or vulnerable ego state cannot hold the direct experience. As a result, the mystical call is then left up to the individual's interpretation, shaped by culture, religion, psychology, and time in history. Essentially, the pure original experience of the archetypal encounter overwhelms the ego and is lost it to the realm of the unconscious where it resides as images, sounds, and symbols.

Put another way, the physical body and the ego structure at this point in human evolution cannot absorb other dimensions of some states of consciousness. As a result, the direct encounter with energy vortexes (archetypes) in the larger cosmos cannot be known firsthand for what it is. Psychologically and physiologically overwhelmed, the aftereffects of the mystical call leave individuals deeply moved and physically impacted, as he or she has been transported beyond the limited five senses of normal waking life. Individuals must now integrate other dimensions of reality, previously unknown, which have carried them into unspeakable realms.

Again, these realms must then be processed through the limitations of one's own life context. The individual is then left with the psychological challenge to interpret the far-reaching experience and integrate it into conscious waking life.

Most people are first aware of an archetypal influence via a physical sensation: raised hair on the back of the neck, shivers down the spine, goose bumps traveling up the arms. A growing physical response commonly occurs and grows stronger when one moves ever more closely to the eye of the archetype. Others experience the archetypal influence through an emotional reaction or the trigger of a personal complex. When the power of the experience overwhelms the ego and normal waking consciousness, it is too difficult to sustain awareness. This is similar to a powerful dream that cannot be held in consciousness upon waking.

Given the intensity, it becomes a kind of conversion experience and, as a result, one develops an unwavering belief in a larger sacred dimension. For some, this verifies their belief in God; for others, the invisible force is reference by many names. For Jung, the magnitude and unspeakable encounter of God as a cosmic force, regardless of what name is used to describe the experience, presented no conflict, either psychologically or religiously.

In fact, it was Jung's encounters with the invisible world of universal patterns that confirmed his belief in a living energy, a responsive source that he freely called God. When asked if he believed in God, Jung responded, "No, I know." Jung saw God as an archetype, a concept that in no way diminishes the power of the God concept as conventionally understood. Rather, he identified God as the powerful, primal, and limitless archetypal living energy source. This vortex of energy, called by many names: God, G-d, Holy Spirit, The Universe, The Sacred, The Gods, Emptiness, The Void, The Numinous, The Holy, The Eternal is known by the aftereffects and how one is forever changed.

The notion of archetypes has yet to be understood by contemporary culture, as much as Jung brought this ancient concept to the modern stage. In its purest direct experience, the meaning of the word has more to do with "primary mold" or original forms and patterns that are known through direct experience from the most subtle dimension of reality known. However, for some philosophers such as Ken Wilber, the archetypal paradigm in Jungian thought is too reductive to understand the true mystical experience since archetypes are characteristically understood in the context of the personal self—even when it paradoxically goes beyond one personal identity to the transpersonal domain. While the transpersonal event carries one beyond one's own personality and into the collective, it still weaves back into the fabric of the actual person and his or her limited identity. According to Wilber, there are many stratas of subtle energy systems that transport one beyond the personal identity or the collective witnessing beyond the self to an absorption with a primordial energy in form. Here, one has a direct experience of unification in formlessness and form.

This dimension of archetypal reality is nondual, multifaceted, and fully merged with a Spirit source that is both in form and formless. Here, the ego-identity or mythic dimensions of archetypal understanding is bypassed. We are no longer dealing with imbedded images of the archetypal hero, crone, mother, witch, etc. that we commonly see in fairy tales, but a subtle energy system of Spirit in which one enters and is absorbed with the manifestation of energy. It is not merely holding a different perspective or serving as a witness to a new reality—one *is* that reality. One is not observing the vast ocean, one *is* the ocean. One is not feeling loving compassion, one *is* loving compassion.

Or depending on the nature of the mystical call, one may pause in the gap between the form and the formless, the subject and the object, and in so doing experience the misery of all humanity, as Indian seer Krishnamurti used to say from his retreat in Ojai, California. (Could this be Jesus' experience from the cross when he asked for the cup to be taken from him?)

From this perspective, there are more dimensions of archetypal reality than we have typically known in the West and must look to the inquiry and practices of sages, seers, and mystics influenced by East to develop a fuller understanding.

Incorporating the Call

Through his investigation of the unconscious world and the role of archetypal influences, Jung understood how his patient's psyche and destiny were shaped. He also recognized that such invisible forces were overwhelming and had dark as well as light influences on the individual psyche. Developing a working relationship with one's unconscious and the archetypal influences that move through the psyche is always required to fulfill the call. To this end, there can only be great respect for the individual who works to tame and integrate these forces. For Jung, this was the exceptional path that required a willingness to forego convention and surrender to the authentic Self.

For those willing to live more mature and individuated lives, there is always a quality of being set apart from the masses, not from an inflated sense of specialness or chosen difference, but through the force of the Higher Allegiance that is given priority and has shaped the personality. This is the wildness that American author Annie Dillard references when she protests, "There is always the temptation in life to diddle around making itsy-bitsy friends and meals and journeys for years on end. It is all so self-conscious, so apparently moral ..." and yet, she (as one who has followed her own daemon), declares, " ...But I won't have it. The world is wilder than that in all directions, more dangerous ... more extravagant and bright. We are … raising tomatoes when we should be raising Cain, or Lazarus."

It is, too, the shared yearning that the poet Oliver Wendell Holmes, Sr., knows when he claims, "On the side of simplicity, I wouldn't give a fig. But for the simplicity on the other side of complexity, for that I would give you anything I have."

Needless to say, despite the brightness and fulfillment that unfolds in living the called life, it is often a lonely one. The very drive that fuels the call and renews personal agency is sparked by something that is otherworldly, and rarely understood by family and friends. Jung understood why and how "walking in shoes too small" many turn their backs on the call. Not everyone tolerates the intensity and complexity of this experience or can process this view behind the veil of normal waking reality, let alone create a new identity, and in Jung's term, *individuate.*

As the life span continues, one must face that the call is not linear or a one-task operation. It is a building of awareness and consciousness, which is an ever-deepening spiral that spans a lifetime. Inner forces (or dragons) lie beyond conscious awareness that may create a fierce battle with the call's demands, with new demons arriving when it seems that the last was slayed.

According to Jung, one's ego strength is, in fact, measured by the innate and accrued ability to contain, tame, endure, negotiate, withstand, and survive the dangers that lurk below the surface in the unconscious realm. The paradox is the guide, for it is a strong ego that allows the descent into the unconscious realm so that one may ascend to new heights. From using the ego to tame and contain the energies and archetypal influences roaming in the unconscious, we become inspired to live beyond its limitations, marked with unsightly repressed wounds, filled with the pus of fear, anger, revenge, and aggression, even as it competes for space with golden unrealized possibilities. This period can be likened to the dark night of the soul, or temptations by the gods, and become a psychological and spiritual battle of monumental proportions.

Therefore, mystical calls may shake the foundations of the conscious ego, use its strength to contain unleashed aspects of material stored in the unconscious realm in which one's entire strength is needed to survive, and take the necessary steps to shift the center of gravity of one's identify to a new and greater Self. To endure the mystical event and complete the assignment, one must also bear up under the weight of what has now broken into consciousness, which may be most threatening to the fragile ego. *We must have a strong ego to risk transcending it.* Bridging the soul dimension to the waking life only deepens as one remembers one's true place in the world, or as the inspired British poet David Whyte reminds us, " To remember the other world in this world is to live in your true inheritance."

While some accept the initial call and enter the road to freedom, some understandably forsake the soul's invitation when the battle is too fierce or lasts too long. This can happen, not only at the beginning of the journey, but at a midpoint or beyond. Shadows live brightly in all of us and require attention throughout our life span. When complex dark feelings are unhinged following a mystical call, the strain of the archetypal grip may be too great.

I wonder if Adolf Hitler, reportedly a sensitive art student at one time, experienced a call that turned dark given his inability to integrate and resolve his aggressive impulses that likely resulted from the abuse of his early life and weak ego structure. Is it possible that Hitler was lost in the grip of an archetypal energy pattern, driving him into madness when he posed as a political shaman to the German masses? Is it possible that Hitler turned his back on a daemon that he could not incorporate—and as a result, lived and died in turmoil and destruction? Dark or misguided calls, which can lead to destruction (as seen in radical religious movements), are yet another reason to decipher mystical calls from a refusal of 'the light that has been seen' and twisted into pathology.

Archetypal energies are powerful and hold unbearable beauty *and* pinching aggression. What attracts can destroy. Even as the "god archetype" has been experienced as energy of love beyond measure, its shadow dimension is destructive, as highlighted in the Old Testament. All that erupts from the mystical call must be integrated into normal waking reality, be it magnificent or horrifying. Managing this and keeping one's own adaptive life skills intact while surrounded by many who may think that you have lost your marbles (while you, in fact, sometimes wonder if you have) is no easy feat. Furthermore, even those who have latched onto the unbounded love and light glimpsed during the call and found a way to say "yes" are not ensured a safe and easy passage. The assignment is an awesome responsibility, and staying true to the glimpse behind the veil is no easy charge. The journey is a hard won passage to the True Self, which always leads to the Divine.

The self that begins is not the Self that arrives. At the outset, we see ourselves one way and claim a particular identity. In fulfilling the call, the self that we thought we were begins to die until "no one" is left. Joyfully, this "no one" is the individuated Real Self that rests in a transcendent sacred reality. It is the place that Christ or the Buddha has beckoned over the centuries—and once known, liberates the soul. The seeking has become the journey and the awareness that the one who was sought has now been found by Another.

Reading Group
Guide: The Meaning
of Mystical Calls

CHAPTER 14

*When love has carried us above all things we receive
in peace the Incomprehensible Light, enfolding us
and penetrating us. What is this Light, if it be not
a contemplation of the Infinite, and an intuition of
Eternity? We behold that which we are, and we are
that which we behold; because our being, without
losing anything of its own personality, is united with
the Divine Truth. . . .* —John of Ruysbroeck

*For now we see through a glass, darkly; but then
face-to-face: now I know in part; but then shall I
know even as also I am known.*
—*1 Corinthians, 13:12*, King James Bible

In hopes of knitting together those with similar experiences,
or reaching others who are curious and value mystical matters,
I offer this summary that can serve as a guide for group discussion.
Whether you are coming out into the light yourself, or listening to
a person who has lived a call—or experienced anything unexplainable, religious or otherwise—exploring the unknown is better with

a companion than without. Use this as a stepping stone to further conversation.

From this study, there are now well-established identifiable characteristics from ancient history to the present.

Historically:
- Mystical calls have been traced from antiquity in both oral and written history.
- The experience occurs in every known culture, race, religion, and tradition across the globe.
- The mystical call not only touches the individual in profound ways, it reaches out to the larger community. The call initiates leadership and ignites increased consciousness for the whole - be it in the form of a shaman, priest, priestess, rabbi, healer, teacher, or artist.

Who is called:
- It is not known why or to whom this occurs, although there are several identifiable shared personality characteristics. They include an uncanny interest in religious or spiritual matters as young children; or an interest in religious services and celebratory rituals, even when there was disinterest or overt disapproval from parents.

Common events occurred prior to being called:
- Reports of accidents, illnesses, episodes of psychological trauma and times of acute stress.

Practical features of the call:
- The call occurred in different physical settings in which an instruction was understood in an audible, visual, or

visceral experience from an encounter with a being, object, or symbol.
- The call was punctuated by strong emotional/affective reactions as well as powerful physiological responses.
- The call catapulted one into an energetic vortex of a loving encounter or cosmos that exceeded anything previously known.
- Some who had previously suffered from physical ailments believed that they were healed during the call.

Observations immediately following the call:
- Following the call, individuals feel disoriented for an average of three days, often with physical symptoms.
- Most experience some form of a religious conversion.
- Acts of synchronicity, which served to offer validation and guidance for the call, were common.
- The frequency and intensity of transpersonal experiences occurred for each person.
- The most common non-rational or transpersonal experiences were psychic premonitions and clairvoyant events.

Shared reflections among those who have been called:
- Acceptance of the call served as an initiation of a personal journey in self-discovery and toward spiritual wisdom.
- An introduction into realms beyond the workings of the conscious personality and material conventions into love-infused realm of the invisible world.
- The power of the call is all consuming, marked by a heightened sense of responsibility, urgency, and desire.
- The time of the mystical experience serves as a major frame of reference in the arc of life; delineating one's life story before and after the call.

- Prior experiences of personal alienation or suffering often provided the groundwork to understand and heed the call.
- The activities, interests, and related tasks that pertain to the call serve as the centerpiece of daily living. Consequently, relationships, friendships, hobbies, and other interests often take a back seat.
- Living a balanced life is always challenging given the demanding nature of the call, as well as the growing passion that continues to develop in living the call.

Changes following the call:
- An orientation toward individual and global suffering that seeks meaning and consciousness from each experience.
- A greater acceptance of all religious faiths and traditions.
- A shift to a nondual state of consciousness, particularly toward one's view of God.
- Increased personal satisfaction and connection to the human family, despite times of loneliness and personal hardship.
- An increased capacity for empathy, feelings of love for others, and a belief that one is held in a universe governed by love.
- A newfound freedom from fear of the future and death's eventuality.

Research findings:
- A growing body of science suggests a wide range of psychological, cognitive, physical, and spiritual changes that occur as a result of mystical experiences, including increases in: cognitive functioning, physical health, capacity to heal, patience, creativity, intuitive sensitivity, interest in serving others, open-mindedness, and greater access and confidence in a cosmic reality.

Tips for the Contemporary Mystic

CHAPTER 15

The greatest responsibility of all: the transmission of the mystery. —Basarab Nicolescu

Calls come in many forms: secular hunches, sacred intuitions, messages from the stranger or closest of intimates, unexpected connections to physical places that reveal themselves as if the very rocks or clouds or sea are speaking. Landscapes, the spoken or written word, art, nature, beauty, and personal intimacy are only a few of the ways the call reaches out to open the heart and gives breath to the unlived life. While this work focuses on the dramatic nature of the mystical call, all calls have meaning and purpose in each life.

This work would not be complete without offering the genuine seeker recommendations for self-care. No doubt, many more prescriptive suggestions exist, but the following guidelines have been gathered from my thirty years of listening to those who have been called, and I hope that they will help you, as well.

- Following any mystical experience, it is important to be gentle with yourself. You are walking on holy ground. Extend a tender hand toward yourself. Rest and sleep.

- Memory is fleeting in this trance-like state. Take notes as you transition back to normal waking consciousness.
- Trust your experience. You are not crazy. In fact, you are most likely evolving into expanded awareness that will make you all the healthier. Many who have had mystical experiences, or sudden strokes of genius, or bolts of out-of-body creativity—or even madness—are evolving in ways that contemporary culture may not yet understand.
- Ask, meditate and pray. Stay open to the call's revelation, even after the initial epiphany. It is always an unfolding process. The assignment may be literal; and/or the assignment may be a symbol that will guide you to a deeper truth. Stay faithful to the unfolding nature of your unique path and its teaching.
- Initially, you may feel frightened or overwhelmed with your assignment. This is very normal. It may go against your plans, hopes, and life dreams. Honor all of the feelings that sweep over you, as more understanding will rise to the surface when you respect your own reactions.
- Pay attention to any and all acts of synchronicity, particularly those that occur immediately after the experience and anything that pertains to your assignment. The Universe is speaking and your job is to be available.
- Remember that rejections and detours have their own wise counsel; allow them to be acts of synchronicity in disguise. The journey is spiral-like and marked by ascents and descents, remembering and forgetting.
- Trust time. The workings of the invisible world, which gripped you, will not abandon you—and when you are ready, new doors of understanding will open. As taught in the *Bhagavad Gita*, that which is bitter becomes so sweet.

- Listen to your day and night dreams. They may be oracles pointing the way.
- Share your story with those who seek self-knowledge and find meaning in the invisible realms.
- If possible, seek out a transpersonal or Jungian therapist, spiritual director, or religious leader who has a frame of reference for spiritual and/or religious experiences. With good fortune, you will find someone willing to explore this with you without an overlay of his or her own beliefs, fears or dogma. If you do not feel seen and supported, do not expose yourself to judgments and misguided prompts. You need a safe place.
- As the mystical aspects of the call are integrated, you will begin to hear the meaning of the assignment as it is meant for your own ears. Once your body nods in agreement, go for it, and receive support from all corners of your life.
- As you act on the assignment, you may receive criticism from those who do not understand. Sometimes you will be abandoned or rejected. This is part of the cost of the quest, but you will endure it. You will discover the strength of your own growing powers and will likely find compassion for others in the face of ridicule or misunderstanding.
- At times, you will be alone on this journey. This, too, is the price of consciousness. The good news is that loneliness is fleeting as you continue to deepen in your understanding of the call's unfolding messages. Increasingly, you will experience solitude as the balm to loneliness and the deep connection you feel with the whole of humanity will become the richest intimacy known. Conversely, some of the strongest feelings of loneliness will be in visiting with others who speak of empty matters.

- The tasks of the call will present circumstances and challenges that will teach you everything you need to learn about the nature of your assignment—and mostly, about yourself.
- Welcome these unknown parts of yourself as a noble guest. Befriend your own suffering without self-pity. Find meaning in your suffering. Inhabit your vulnerability.
- Listen to the call throughout your life span. Destiny is always unfolding; waiting in the bud of our DNA; made increasingly conscious through the mystical call.
- Remember that it is never too late to heed the beckoning of the mystical call. In fact, abandoning the call may have been the only thing you could have done, and that delay now serves as the needed preparation for fulfilling it in brilliant form.
- Remember that you walk in and between this world and others. Remember that you are part of a larger mysterious tribe. We are always looking for you, ready to embrace you, both now and forever.

Afterword

The normal way never leads home.
—John O'Donohue

Working through personal demons becomes the gritty sand that makes the best inner pearls. In living the call, the perfect situations and circumstances will present themselves to stir up that which has been repressed and acted out in neurotic ways. You are given an opportunity to heal this inner place and in so doing, will be more skillfully prepared for the assignment. It will, no doubt, require you to stand apart from convention and claim the authentic Self to carry the light into the larger world. From this place, the spacious heart holds all doors open and welcomes the stranger, beginning with yourself.

Those who are not able to surrender to the call have an understandable burden to bear. You may suffer and feel lost, riddled with doubt, aching from self-betrayal and agitated entrapment. Some jump ship, seduced by money, status or power. For others, the endless demands of raising a family and managing the disapproval of others will leave them feeling defeated. Most poignant is the grief felt in relationship with the unnamed holy longing; an unquenchable desire to be in dialogue with the wisdom of the ancestors. Still, there is meaning to be found in this place, too. Mercy is great and redemption steadfast, as Mystery waits for us all. Blinded by how we have exalted that which is false, the voice (while muffled) remains.

For those who accept the assignment of the gods, the power and promise of the mystical call is the beginning of a new life, a growing participation with Mystery that was previously unknown. Cultural and societal norms hold less and less sway on the individual. Expect a heightened level of creativity, urgency, and access to the unconscious world of intuition, dreams, symbols, and images pointing to that which is moving and growing within. Here, the soul's wisdom and the authentic Self reach beyond the limitations of the personality.

All language to testify to a God encounter can, at best, serve only as parable, symbol, or metaphor, given the power of the experience. Using the term "archetypes" interchangeably with God language may be difficult, even offensive, to some readers, but truth transcends language, cultural habits, interpretations, and dearest held convictions. Consequently, when patterns of energy point to "God," there is no need for a split between science and soul. The word "archetype" merely points to the energy of Mystery as it is experienced in deeper ways and called by many names. The Sacred Source becomes The All, The Numinous, The Unnamable, Yahweh, Unsynonymous, Void, Eternal, Wholly Other, Infinite, Unknowable and God—and many more.

Ultimately, whatever word used reflects the energy of a relationship that gives life, carries us from dust to dust in a flicker of time, infuses us with love, calls us to know the Self, and lives in relationship with the Divine Source. In a most personal way, the mystical life engages in relationship with God as if in combat at times, locked into a stranglehold, encountering a Holy and Terrible Energy, which erupts, intrudes, cuts into personal and global history in the time-space continuum. The call in this context is a living dynamic relationship with a steadfast wild force, no different than if we faced a hungry tiger, bowed before a lightning bolt, or asked for mercy in the face of a catastrophic wind. This nameless force is incomprehensible to the human mind. It is a furious and never failing energy that is best recognized in the power of love.

Despite the seduction of the material life, God roars down, creating form and chaos as the soul evolves. There is no room for an indifferent attitude after the God encounter has occurred. To turn away may describe the very nature of sin: a betrayal of divine love; a denial of the covenantal dialogue with one's destiny. It is the ultimate altar call.

A changing perspective of our individual and collective history takes a different shape as the journey is deepened into new form. No longer are we seen as prisoners, but as souls who are moving toward liberation. We walk on centuries of dust and bones, honoring those who have struggled and given life to us. We are in constant dialogue with an ancient witness that breathes into our efforts to wake up the earth while we walk among it. Each moment is an invitation to say "yes" and arrive as poet William Blake described so eloquently:

"I give you the end of a golden string;
Only wind it into a ball,
It will lead you in at Heaven's gate—
Built in Jerusalem's wall."

In closing, many years have now passed since the first rumpled index card was written, and many decades since a young girl sought to understand the voice of God. Today, thousands of stories have been heard and recognized, thousands of lives witnessed as divine tumult has shown itself through visions and voices from the unseen world. Individuals, like many of you reading this book, have participated in a history of humanity: glimpsing the face of Mystery and surviving. With each glance, human history is ever quickened in its velocity as individual souls cry out for meaning and significance to serve the world in need.

Together we serve this wild and gentle planet in all its brilliance and brokenness, and in so doing are shattered and recreated anew. Perhaps every life is a Spirit-journey that follows the path to Golgotha or Mecca or The Temple Mount, reaching out to others even as the movement is healing one's own heart and saving one's own soul. This is the resounding *yes* that has made all the difference. It is the sound of a soul becoming free. It has been a most magnificent obsession.

Abbreviated Glossary
of Jungian Terms

ANIMA: the feminine aspect of the masculine psyche. They are those qualities a man seeks in a woman [or projects onto a woman] whom he perceives as his "soul mate" because she expresses for him that which he has not yet accepted and expressed of himself.

ANIMUS: the masculine aspects of the feminine psyche such as creativity, intellectualism, aggression, etc. In dreams and imagination it can take many forms; eg., hero, sage, Don Juan, protector, etc. As with men's anima, the *animus* is projected onto real men.

ARCHETYPES: the symbols and concepts we "know" because they have been and are common to all of humankind. They are patterns that live inside and outside of us. They encompass instincts and images, motifs and physical reactions. Example: *mother* symbolizes nurturing, loving, protection, etc., and goes beyond the personal experience of mother. Increasingly, it is believed that there are many subtle dimensions to archetypal reality.

COLLECTIVE UNCONSCIOUS: a universal storehouse of knowledge and patterned perceptions, which are inherited and present at birth. It contains all the myths, superstitions, and markings of our ancestors. It is manifested in archetypal symbols and rarely becomes conscious.

COMPLEX: for Jung, a *complex* is an independent cluster of ideas, attitudes and/or motives that have been split off from the rest of the psyche and lead a more or less autonomous existence. Complexes normally work outside of consciousness and must be made conscious in order to be changed. Individuals may harbor several complexes that become competitive. It is a vortex of psychic energy that draws much psychic material into its sphere of influence with one or more emotionally loaded archetypes at its core. One's life can be structured around the demands of these archetypes.

CREATIVE COMPLEX: a complex that is focused on a creative process such as painting, poetry, sculpture, architecture, dance, etc.

EGO: that which represents what I call myself. It is the center of consciousness.

INDIVIDUATION: a process of becoming the individual that exists in one's innate blueprint, the inherited potential. This is a lifelong journey and the essence of analysis.

PERSONA: the mask that I wear to show to the world.

PERSONAL UNCONSCIOUS: that part of the psyche where unnoticed and/or unpleasant personal feelings and experiences have been deposited and, as yet, uncalled upon capabilities and ideas are hidden. These can be made conscious through free association, hypnosis, psychotherapy, etc.

SELF: the center of the entire psyche. Can be called God. It transcends any and all particular aspects of the person and makes the person unique; i.e., the whole is more than the sum of its parts.

SHADOW: the negative or repressed aspects of the unconscious; that psychological material that cannot be faced and incorporated into awareness.

Sources

Chapter 1

Robert A. Johnson, *Inner Work: Using Dreams and Active Imagination for Personal Growth* (New York: HarperCollins Publishers, 2009).

Chapter 3

Mary Oliver, "The Summer Day," *House of Light* (Beacon Press, 1992).

Chapter 4

D.W. Winnicott, *Playing and Reality* (Penguin, 1971).
Antoine de Saint Exupéry, *The Little Prince* (New York: Harcourt Inc., 1943).
P.M.H. Atwater, *Near-Death Experiences, The Rest of the Story: What They Teach Us About Living, Dying, and Our True Purpose* (Charlottesville, VA: Hampton Roads, 2011).

Chapter 5

C.G. Jung, *Modern Man in Search of a Soul*, trans. W.S. Dell and Cary F. Bayes. (New York: Harcourt Brace Jovanovich, 1955).

Robert Powell, ed. *The Nectar of Immortality: Sri Nisargadatta Maharaj's Discourses on the Eternal* (San Diego: Blue Dove Press, 1966).

Chapter 6

Mircea Eliade, *A History of Religious Ideas: From the Stone Age to the Eleusinian Mysteries* (Chicago: University of Chicago Press, 1978).

Chapter 7

P.M.H. Atwater, *Near-Death Experiences, The Rest of the Story: What They Teach Us About Living, Dying, and Our True Purpose* (Charlottesville, VA: Hampton Roads, 2011).

Robert Powell, ed. *The Nectar of Immortality: Sri Nisargadatta Maharaj, Discourses on the Eternal* (San Diego: Blue Dove Press, 1966).

Ashhok Bedi, *Crossing the Healing Zone from Illness to Wellness* (Lake Worth, FL: Ibis Press, 2013).

Evelyn Underhill, *The Essentials of Mysticism* (Oxford: One World Publications, 1999).

Mircea Eliade, *A History of Religious Ideas: From the Stone Age to the Eleusinian Mysteries* (Chicago: University of Chicago Press, 1978).

Bustan of Saadi, *Complete Works* (Los Angeles: Indo-European Publishing, 2012).

Chapter 8

Gregory Vlastos, *Socrates: Ironist and Moral Philosopher* (Ithaca: Cornell University Press, 1991).

Martin Bell, *Distant Fire* (San Francisco: Harper & Row, 1971).

Chapter 9

P.M.H. Atwater, *Near-Death Experiences, The Rest of the Story: What They Teach Us About Living, Dying, and Our True Purpose* (Charlottesville, VA: Hampton Roads, 2011).

Meister Eckart, *Complete Works of Meister Eckart* (New York: Crossroads Publishing, 1992).

Flower Newhouse, *Mysticism: The Collected Works of Flower A. Newhouse* Vol. I.

Andrew Harvey, *The Essential Mystics* (San Francisco: HarperCollins, 1999).

Richard Rohr, *Immortal Diamond: The Search for Our True Self* (San Francisco: Jossey-Bass, 2013).

Chapter 11

Evelyn Underhill, The Essentials of Mysticism (Oxford: One World Publications, 1999).

T.S. Eliot, *Little Gidding* (San Diego: Harcourt, 1943).

Evelyn Underhill, *Mysticism, A Study in the Nature and Development of Spiritual Consciousness* (Mineola: Dover Publications, Inc., 2002).

Raphael Brown, *The Little Flowers of St. Francis* (New York: Bantam Doubleday, 1958).

Raymond Moody's seminal work in near death experiences (NDE) identifies nineteen key elements, most of which are reported after mystical calls.

P.M.H. Atwater, *Near-Death Experiences, The Rest of the Story: What They Teach Us About Living, Dying, and Our True Purpose* (Charlottesville, VA: Hampton Roads, 2011).

Robert Powell, ed. *The Nectar of Immortality: Sri Nisargadatta Maharaj's Discourses on the Eternal* (San Diego: Blue Dove Press, 1966).

Martin Bell, *Distant Fire* (San Francisco: Harper & Row, 1971).

Jack Jezreel, "To Love Without Exception," "Perfection," *Oneing*, vol. 4, no. 1 (Albuquerque, NM: Center for Action and Contemplation, 2016).

Alan Watts, The Spirit of Zen (New York, New York: Grove Press, 1958).

Chapter 12

Russell Shorto, *Saints and Madmen* (New York: Henry Holt and Company, 1999).

Gary Zukav, *The Seat of the Soul* (New York: Simon & Schuster Inc., 1989).

Dean Hamer, *The God Gene: How Faith Is Hardwired into Our Genes* (New York: Doubleday, 2004).

William James, *The Varieties of Religious Experience* (Cambridge, Mass: Harvard University Press, 1985).

Kaja Pervina, "The Mad Genius Mystery," *Psychology Today*, July/August 2017: Volume 50, No. 4.

C.G. Jung, *Modern man in search of a soul*, trans. W.S. Dell and Cary F. Baynes. (New York: Harcourt Brace Jovanovich, Publishers, 1933).

Anne Sexton, *The Awful Rowing Towards God* (Boston: Houghton Mifflin Co., 1975).

Ken Wilber, *The Essential Ken Wilber* (Boston: Shambhala, 1998).

Further Reading

Anderson, Bernhard W. *Understanding the Old Testament*. Englewood Cliffs, New Jersey: Prentice-Hall, Inc., 1975.

Barks, Coleman, and Michael Green. *The Illuminated Rumi*. New York: Broadway Books, 1997.

Barnett, M. "Spiritual masters: An Interview with William Segal." *Parabola* 25(3), (Fall 2000): 11–19. California Sage Publications, Inc.

Bedi, Ashok. *Crossing the Healing Zone*. Lake Worth, FL: Ibis Press, 2013.

Bond, A. *Christ-Centered Mysticism*. Toronto, 1959.

Bellah, Robert; Richard Madsen; William Sullivan; Ann Swidler; and Steven Tipton. *Habits of the Heart*. New York: Harper & Row, 1985.

Bernbaum, John, and Simon Steer. *Why Work?* Grand Rapids: Baker Book House, 1986.

Boggs, W. H., Jr. *All Ye Who Labor*. Richmond: John Knox Press, 1962.

Brewi, Janice, and Anne Brennan. *Mid-life Spirituality and Jungian Archetypes*. York Beach, Maine: Nicholas Hays, 1999.

Bromiley, Geoffrey (Ed.). *The International Standard Bible Encyclopedia* (Vol. 1). Grand Rapids: William B. Eerdmans, 1979.

Brunner, Emil. *The Divine Imperative*. Philadelphia: Westminster Press, 1947.

Burnham, Sophy. *The Ecstatic Journey: The Transforming Power of Mystical Experience.* New York: Ballantine Books, 1997.

Campbell, Joseph. *The Masks of God: Occidental Mythology.* New York: Penguin Books, 1977.

Cheney, Sheldon. *Men Who Have Walked with God.* Montana: Kessinger Publishing Company, 1945.

Connell, Jan. *Queen of the Cosmos: Interviews with the Visionaries of Medjugorje.* Brewster, Mass.: Parachute Press, 1990.

Corbett, Lionel. *The Religious Function of the Psyche.* New York: Routledge Publishing, 1996.

Cousineau, Phil, and Stuart L. Brown, Eds. *A Hero's Journey: Joseph Campbell on His Life and Work.* New York: Harper and Row, 1990.

Creedon, Jeremiah. "God With a Million Faces." *Utne Reader* 88 (July/August 1998): 42–48.

Dixon-Kolar, Robert. "Bending and Turning: The Lessons of Shaker Craft." *Parabola* 25(3) (Fall 2000): 20–25.

Dols, W. "Understanding Life Backwards." *The Bible Workbench* (Winter 1998): 2–7.

Dossey, Larry. *Reinventing Medicine.* San Francisco: HarperCollins, 1999.

Dwinell, Michael. *God-birthing: Toward Sacredness, Personal Meaning, and Spiritual Nourishment.* Liguori, Missouri: Triumph Books, 1994.

Eliade, Mircea. *A History of Religious Ideas: From the Stone Age to the Eleusinian Mysteries.* Translated by W. R. Trask. Chicago: University of Chicago Press, 1982 (Orig. publ. 1978).

Eliade, Mircea. *A History of Religious Ideas: From Gautama Buddha to the Triumph of Christianity.* Translated by W.R. Trask. Chicago: University of Chicago Press, 1982 (Orig. publ. 1978).

Eliade, Mircea. *Rites and Symbols of Initiation.* New York: Harper & Row, 1958.

Epstein, Gerald. *Climbing Jacob's ladder: Finding Spiritual Freedom Through the Stories of the Bible.* New York: ACMI Press, 1999.

Fox, Adam. *Dean Inge*. London: John Mundy, 1980.

Fromm, Erich. *Escape from Freedom*. New York: Penguin Books, 1941.

Grof, Stanislav. *Realms of the Human Unconscious: Observations from Research*. New York: E.P. Dutton, 1976.

Guba, E., & Lincoln, Y. "Competing paradigms in qualitative research." In N. Denzin & Y. Lincoln (Eds.), Handbook of Qualitative Research (1994): 105–17.

Hardy, Lee. *The Fabric of this World*. Grand Rapids, MI: William B. Eerdmans, 1990.

Harvey, Andrew. *Teachings of Rumi*. Boston: Shambhala, 1999.

Harvey, Andrew. *The Essential Mystics*. San Francisco: HarperCollins Publishers, 1996.

Hillman, James. *Insearch: Psychology and Religion*. New York: Harper Collins Publishers, Inc., 1997.

Hillman, James. "Pathologizing (or falling apart)." Terry Lectures. Yale University, 1972. New York: Harper & Row.

Hillman, James. "Psychologizing." Terry Lectures. Yale University, 1972. New York: Harper & Row.

Hillman, James. *The Thought of the Heart and the Soul of the World*. Woodstock, CT: Spring Publications, 1995.

Hodge, David R. "Spiritual Ecomaps: A New Diagrammatic Tool for Assessing Marital and Family Spirituality." *Journal of Marital and Family Therapy* 26 (2) (April 2000): 217–28.

Holland, John L. *The Psychology of Vocational Choice*. Waltham, MA: Blaisdell Publications, 1966.

Homan, K. B. "Vocation as the quest for authentic existence." *The Career Development Quarterly* (1986): 14–23.

Jacobi, Jolande. *The Philosophy of C.G. Jung*. New Haven, CT: Yale University Press, 1973.

James, William. *The Varieties of Religious Experience*. Cambridge, Mass: Harvard University Press, 1985.

Jung, C.G. *Aion: Researches into the Phenomenology of the Self.* Translated by R.F.C. Hull. Princeton, NJ: Princeton University Press, 1959.

Jung, C.G. "Answer to Job." *Collected Work* (Vol. 8). Princeton, NJ: Princeton University Press, 1973.

Jung, C.G. *Analytical Psychology, its Theory and Practice.* New York: Random House, 1968.

Jung, C.G. *Aspects of the Feminine.* Translated by R.F.C. Hull. Princeton, NJ: Princeton University Press, 1982.

Jung, C.G. *Aspects of the Masculine.* Translated by R.F.C. Hull. Princeton, NJ: Princeton University Press, 1991.

Jung, C.G. *The Integration of the Personality.* New York: Farrar & Reinhart, Inc., 1939.

Jung, C.G. *The Psychology of Kundalini Yoga.* Translated by Sonu Shamdasani. Princeton, NJ: Princeton University Press, 1996.

Jung, C.G. *Modern Man in Search of a Soul.* Translated by W.S. Dell and Cary F. Bayne. New York: Harcourt Brace Jovanovich, Publishers, 1933.

Jung, C.G. *Mysterium Coniunctionis.* Translated by R.F.C. Hull. Princeton, NJ: Princeton University Press, 1989.

Jung, C.G. *Psychology and Religion: West and East* (2nd ed). Translated by R.F.C. Hull. Princeton, NJ: Princeton University Press, 1969. (Original pub. 1958).

Jung, C.G. *The Psychogenesis of Mental Disease.* Translated by R.F.C. Hull. Princeton, NJ: Princeton University Press, 1989.

Jung, C.G. *Psychology of the Unconscious. The Collected Works of C.G. Jung.* (Supplementary Vol. B). Translated by Beatrice M. Hinkle. Princeton, NJ: Princeton University Press, 1991.

Jung, C.G. *The Archetypes and the Collective Unconscious.* Translated by R.F.C. Hull. Princeton, NJ: Princeton University Press, 1977.

Kavanaugh, Kieran, and Otilio Rodriguez, Translators. *The Collected Work of St. John of the Cross.* Washington, D.C.: Institute of Carmelite Studies, 1979.

Kildahl, John P. "The Hazards of High Calling." *Pastoral Psychology* 12 (1961): 41–46.

Kohák, Erazim. "Existence and the phenomenological epoché." *Journal of Existentialism* 8 (1967): 19–47.

Leclercq, C. *The Religious Vocation*. New York: P.J. Kennedy and Sons, 1955.

Lesage, Germain. *Personalism and Vocation*. New York: Alba House, 1966.

Lewis, Roy. *Choosing your Career, Finding your Vocation*. New York: Paulist Press, 1989.

Levoy, Gregg. *Callings: Finding and Following an Authentic Life*. New York: Harmony Books, 1997.

Margolis, Robert, and Kirk Elifson. "A Typology of Religious Experience." *Journal for the Scientific Study of Religion* 18 (1979): 61–67.

Matousek, Mark. "Up Close and Transpersonal: Ken Wilber." *Utne Reader* 88 (July/August 1998): 50–55, 106–07.

Matousek, Mark. "Should you design your own religion?" *Utne Reader* 88 (July/August 1998): 44–48.

Middleton, Robert G. "Revising the concept of vocation for the Industrial Age." *Christian Century* 103 (1986): 943–45.

Miller, Samuel. "The Mystery of our Calling." *Pastoral Psychology* 16 (1965): 37–42.

Moustakas, Clark. *Heuristic Research: Design, Methodology, and Applications*. Newbury Park, CA: SAGE Publishing, 1990.

O'Brien, Elmer. *Varieties of Mystic Experience*. New York: Mentor–Omega Books, 1964.

Oliver, Mary. *House of Light*. Boston, MA: Beacon Press, 1990.

Otto, R. *The Idea of the Holy*. New York: Oxford University Press, 1963.

Pankratz, L.D. & Pankratz, D. M. "Determinants in choosing a nursing career." *Nursing Research* 18 (1969): 263–67.

Pearson, Carol. *The Hero Within: Six Archetypes We Live By*. San Francisco: Harper & Row, 1986.

Perry, John W. *The Self in Psychotic Process*. Berkeley, CA: University of California Press, 1953.

Perry, John W. *The Far Side of Madness*. Englewood Cliffs, NJ: Prentice-Hall, 1974.

Pike, Nelson. *Mystic Union, an Essay in the Phenomenology of Mysticism*. Ithaca, NY: Cornell University Press, 1992.

Reason & Rowan, eds. *Human Inquiry: A Sourcebook of New Paradigm Research*, 208–17 and 458–71. Westchester: John Wiley & Sons, 1981.

Roe, Anne. *The Psychology of Occupations*. New York: Wiley, 1956.

Samuels, Andrew. *Politics and the Couch*. New York: Other Press, 2001.

Shorto, Russell. *Saints and Madmen*. New York: Henry Holt and Company, 1999.

Sikora, J.J. *Calling*. New York: Herder and Herder, 1968.

Sikora, J.J. *The Christian Intellect and the Mystery of Being*. The Hague: Martinus Nijhoff, 1966.

Sinetar, Marsha. *Do What You Love, the Money will Follow*. New York: Paulist Press, 1987.

Singer, June. *Boundaries of the Soul*. Garden City: Doubleday & Co., 1972

Smith, Huston. *Why Religion Matters*. San Francisco: Harper Collins, 2001.

Smith, Huston. *Cleansing the Doors of Perception*. New York: Penguin Putnam, 2000.

Smoley, Richard. "The Source of Wisdom." *Parabola* 25(3) (August 2000): 6–10.

Sobosan, J.G. "A Voice Within: The Prophetic Experience of Vocation." *Journal of Religion and* Health 24 (1985): 125–32.

Spinks, G. Stephens. *Psychology and Religion: An Introduction to Contemporary Views*. Boston: Beacon Press, 1963.

Stark, Rodney. "A Taxonomy of Religious Experience." *Journal for the Scientific Study of Religion* 5 (1965): 97–116.

Stefflre, Buford. "Vocational Development: Ten Propositions in Search of a Theory." *The Personnel and Guidance Journal* 44 (1966): 611–16.

Storr, Anthony. *Feet of Clay: Saints, Sinners, and Madmen, a Study of Gurus.* New York: The Free Press, 1996.

Storr, Anthony (Ed.). *The Essential Jung.* Princeton, NJ: Princeton University Press, 1983.

Trueblood, Elton. *Your Other Vocation.* New York: Harper & Brothers, 1952.

Underhill, Evelyn. *The Essentials of Mysticism* (2nd ed.). Oxford: One World Publications, 1999.

van Manen, Max. *Researching Lived Experience: Human Science for an Action Sensitive Pedagogy.* Albany, NY: State University of New York Press, 1990.

Vetter, Herbert (Ed.). *The Heart of God.* Boston: Tuttle, 1998.

Warnath, Charles. "Vocational Theories: Direction to Nowhere." *The Personnel and Guidance Journal* 53 (1975): 422–28.

Wauck, LeRoy. (Ed.). *The Psychology of Religious Vocations.* Lanham, MD: University Press of America, 1983.

Weatherhead, Leslie D. *After Death.* London: The Epworth Press, 1956.

Webster's Ninth New Collegiate Dictionary. Springfield, MA: Merriam-Webster, Inc., 1987.

Weller, Francis. *The Wild Edge of Sorrow.* Berkeley, CA: North Atlantic Books, 2015.

Wilber, Ken. *The Essential Ken Wilber.* Boston: Shambhala, 1998.

Wingren, Gustaf. *Luther on Vocation.* Philadelphia: Muhlenberg Press, 1957.

Wise, Carroll. "The call to the ministry." *Pastoral Psychology* 9 (1958): 9–17.

Acknowledgments

Nearly all of the cherished mentors and friends who guided and supported me through the original research and dissertation are now in spirit. This only highlights the temporal nature of our brief days. Their legacies are ever present and continue to fill me with gratitude.

Huston Smith served as a spiritual guide and supportive father figure when I needed him the most. Jeanne Loomer, friend and mentor, possessed an everyday common sense infused with wisdom. I'll never forget Jeanne's simple warning on the eve of my ministerial vows: "Remember, after tomorrow, you are never again one of the boys (or girls)."

Deln Dreffin, steadfast gentle spirit, modeled feminine grace in an ever-changing world. Joseph Fabry in partnership with Victor Frankl taught me to probe the healing revelation of meaning at every turn. Marilyn Jenai whispered "go inside" with each unanswered question. Terry Sloan served as a loving companion, colleague and mentor in ministry and social justice; the depths of his influence grasped only in hindsight. Avian Rogers quieted the longing after so many restless years, bridging the body with spirit in necessary ways.

If I could speak now to all of them, I'd say: Through all of your rare and illumined gifts, I have learned to trust the integrity of my own voice and stay true to the light that I have seen. Your presence echoes through these pages and my heartfelt gratitude only grows with the passing years.

I had nary a clue of what would be asked of me in rewriting an academic project into a readable nonacademic manuscript, so I must thank friend and writer Joan Alden who encouraged me in this final stretch. And then, there's trailblazing Phil Cousineau: writer, photographer, filmmaker, and friend, whose creative fire is only overshadowed by his big heart. Phil has the rare capacity to inspire even the most tentative writer all the way to publication. To Alan Maltz, whose photograph *The Calling* not only makes this a most fitting and beautiful cover to this book but blesses me in my home each day. Alan knows what is means to be called and lives it through the camera's lens, bringing nature's beauty to all who can bear the brightness.

I am indebted to David Codding and Leslie Smukler, godparents extraordinaire, who read stories to sleepy eyes and noticed when the dishes piled high. David, had I realized your days were few, I would not have asked so much or been as preoccupied with this work. Each call exacts its price and, now, your spirit with Time's arrow remains forever in my heart.

For every person who has shared stories of the invisible world over these many decades with me, this is for you. Some will recognize your story, paraphrased to illustrate a particular quality or feature. Others will recognize your experiences woven or collapsed into other stories to highlight the essence of the subject considered. I have tried to paraphrase, compile, and hone in on your experiences while staying true to the intent of what you communicated. Without you, this book would not exist. The tribe is strong and I am grateful.

About the Author

Danielle Green, Ph.D., has earned a Masters and Doctorate in Psychology as well as a Masters of Divinity. In addition to being trained in Jungian Psychology (Ph.D.), her expertise includes training in the fields of Family Therapy, Hypnosis, Neurofeedback, Trauma, Attachment Disorders, Mood Disorders, Psychodrama, Imago Therapy for Couples, and the Enneagram.

Dr. Green is also an ordained Unitarian Universalist minister and a Spiritual Director. Her research interests include transgenerational family therapy, altered states of consciousness, dream analysis, and the interfacing of psychoanalysis and mysticism as a transformative experience.

Prior to entering private practice, Dr. Green was the founding Director of Safe Place and Rape Crisis Center (Sarasota, FL) and psychotherapist at New College (Sarasota) and the Stanford Research Institute (Menlo Park, CA). Dr. Green has worked in private practice in Berkeley, Sarasota, and London. She continues to lecture and facilitate groups and retreats throughout the United States, Europe, and India.

CPSIA information can be obtained
at www.ICGtesting.com
Printed in the USA
BVHW031153290123
657377BV00006B/73

9 781480 870109